Exploring Altcoins and the Next Crypto Wave

Altcoins: Investing in the Future of Cryptocurrencies

Ariana Reyes

Table of Contents

INTRODUCTION

The rise of cryptocurrencies has been nothing short of revolutionary in the world of finance and technology, which is constantly shifting and developing. While Bitcoin was the first cryptocurrency, the advent of other cryptocurrencies, often known as "altcoins," has further enriched the field. These cryptocurrencies look into a future in which blockchain technology will change sectors in ways we cannot even imagine.

Welcome to "Exploring Altcoins and the Next Crypto Wave: Altcoins- Investing in the Future of Cryptocurrencies." This e-book will serve as your all-encompassing guide to comprehending the world of altcoins and how those cryptocurrencies reshape the future of investment and finance. This e-book is designed to provide you the knowledge and insights you need to navigate the complex and exciting world of altcoin investments, regardless of whether you are a seasoned crypto enthusiast or just beginning your adventure into the world of digital assets.

A decentralized digital asset class that challenged existing financial systems and introduced the concept of a trustless, peer-to-peer currency, cryptocurrencies came into being with the creation of Bitcoin in 2009. This event is considered to be the birth of cryptocurrencies. The success of Bitcoin demonstrates the potential for blockchain technology to transform how we manage transactions and transfer value. As Bitcoin's popularity continued to grow, it made way for the developing of a wide variety of alternative coins (altcoins). Each cryptocurrency is intended to solve a unique problem within the decentralized ecosystem and open up new opportunities.

Even while Bitcoin is still the most widely used cryptocurrency, its limits have become more evident throughout its history. Innovative minds were motivated to look for other options because of problems with scalability, transaction speed, and a lack of smart contract capability. As a result, alternative coins came into existence to resolve the issues mentioned earlier and bring new capabilities to the blockchain industry. As a direct consequence, a thriving ecosystem of alternative coins has emerged, providing cryptocurrency enthusiasts and investors with various options beyond Bitcoin.

Alternative coins are not only Bitcoin imitations; they are the product of a creative fusion of technological advancement and financial innovation. They introduce smart contracts, cross-chain interoperability, decentralized apps (DApps), and more. The variety of cryptocurrencies known as altcoins is analogous to various applications that could be developed with blockchain technology. These applications range from changing property rights with non-fungible tokens (NFTs) to upending the financial services industry with decentralized finance (DeFi). Individuals have the option to support initiatives that are in line with their ideals while at the same time increasing their chances of profiting from the advancement of technology if they invest in alternative coins.

In the following chapters of this e-book, we will delve deeply into the world of alternative coins (altcoins), investigating their myriad categories, investment possibilities, methods for studying and analyzing projects, and the most important market players. In addition, we will address the challenges and risks connected with investing in altcoins, and we will help you develop an informed investment strategy tailored to your objectives and level of comfort with risk.

Join us on this journey as we uncover the intricacies of altcoins and explore how they shape the future of cryptocurrencies and investments. Whether you are interested in the most recent trends in altcoins, seeking to diversify your investment portfolio, or intrigued by the transformative potential of blockchain technology, you are sure to find something to pique your interest here. This is the first step on your journey to becoming a knowledgeable altcoin investor.

CHAPTER I

Understanding Altcoins

Defining Altcoins: Beyond Bitcoin

Bitcoin's towering influence has unquestionably cast a long shadow over the landscape of the cryptocurrency industry, which is continuously expanding. The term "cryptocurrency" has practically become synonymous with Bitcoin's name due to Bitcoin's status as the revolutionary digital currency that served as the "poster child" for the movement toward digital currencies. However, the history of digital currencies does not finish with Bitcoin; instead, it is merely the beginning of a more comprehensive narrative that embraces a wide variety of digital assets known as "altcoins."

Altcoins, short for "alternative coins," are a fascinating and diverse part of cryptocurrencies. Altcoins have gone far beyond the confines of ordinary currency, pushing into new terrain with unique features, capabilities, and use cases. While they do have a common basis with Bitcoin, the underlying blockchain technology, altcoins, has gone far beyond the boundaries of simple currency.

An alternative coin, or altcoin, refers to any digital asset that is not Bitcoin. Even though this term would appear to be basic, it actually comprises an astonishing diversity of projects, each of which has its own distinctive qualities and objectives. These alternative coins might be viewed as digital experiments that push the frontiers of blockchain technology and pose a challenge to the status quo that Bitcoin has created. They have made the environment of cryptocurrencies more diverse, providing users and investors with a rich tapestry of alternatives that go beyond the digital gold that was initially offered.

Alternate coins are frequently classified into distinct categories according to the functions and characteristics that they offer. Platform altcoins are a notable example of a prominent category. Ethereum, which is currently the second largest cryptocurrency in terms of market capitalization, was the first cryptocurrency to pioneer this category by introducing the idea of smart contracts and decentralized applications (DApps). These alternative coins work as platforms on which programmers may create a wide variety of applications, ranging from decentralized finance (DeFi) protocols to non-fungible token (NFT) marketplaces. This encourages creativity and broadens the use of blockchain technology beyond the realm of basic transactions.

Another interesting category of alternative coins is known as "privacy coins." These coins were developed in response to one of the most noticeable drawbacks of Bitcoin, which is that Bitcoin transactions cannot be conducted in complete anonymity. Users of cryptocurrencies such as Monero, Zcash, and Dash are able to transact without publicly disclosing the amounts of their transactions or the addresses they use since these cryptocurrencies make use of sophisticated cryptographic mechanisms. These alternative coins cater to consumers who place a high value on increased privacy and fungibility, two features that Bitcoin's transparent ledger makes it difficult for it to deliver.

In addition, alternative coins are frequently linked to particular use cases that illustrate the wide range of industries that could take advantage of blockchain technology. Take, for example, the cryptocurrency known as Ripple (XRP), which is designed specifically for making swift international payments. The fact that it prioritizes the facilitation of quick and inexpensive international transactions has drawn the attention of financial institutions all over the world. In a similar vein, Cardano (ADA) places an emphasis on research-driven development and aspires to establish a blockchain platform that is both sustainable and scalable for the creation of a wide range of applications.

Alternate coins came into existence as a result of the process of forking. Forking is the process by which the codebase of a cryptocurrency is split into two independent entities. This is typically done as a result of differences within the community on the path that the project will take in the future. The most well-known instance of forking is the division of the Bitcoin cryptocurrency, which led to the launch of Bitcoin Cash (BCH) and, subsequently, Bitcoin SV (BSV). These alternative coins came into existence with different block sizes and other technical improvements, all of which were made to address difficulties with scalability and transaction speed.

The world of alternative coins is not without its fair share of controversies and difficulties. There are currently hundreds of alternative coins available, and some critics believe that the market is already oversaturated with initiatives that do not offer genuine value or innovation. In addition, the proliferation of fraudulent initial coin offerings (ICOs) and other frauds has forced regulatory agencies to tighten their grip on the cryptocurrency field.

This has produced an atmosphere in which investors are required to conduct extensive due diligence in order to avoid being taken advantage of.

In conclusion, altcoins are a fascinating and indispensable component of the ecosystem that surrounds cryptocurrencies. They are examples of the countless opportunities that can be created by blockchain technology, which go well beyond Bitcoin's initial concept. These digital assets give a vivid picture of the ever-changing world, from platform altcoins that encourage innovation to privacy coins that enhance the anonymity of transactional activity. Even while the world of cryptocurrencies is always changing, there is one thing that can be said with absolute certainty: the history of altcoins is a story that goes beyond Bitcoin and will have a significant impact on the future of finance, technology, and digital innovation.

Differentiating Altcoins from Bitcoin

Bitcoin reigns as the unquestioned pioneer in the wide realm of cryptocurrencies. It has captured the interest of people all over the world since it was the first decentralized digital currency. The enigmatic figure known only as "Satoshi Nakamoto" initiated its production in 2009, marking the beginning of an innovative concept that posed a threat to conventional financial systems. On the other hand, as the ecosystem of cryptocurrencies continued to develop, Bitcoin was no longer the only competitor in the market. The proliferation of altcoins, also known as alternative cryptocurrencies, brought a new facet to the industry, since each coin has its own set of distinguishing characteristics, functions, and value propositions. To successfully manage the complexities of this ever-evolving market, it is crucial to have a solid grasp of the differences that exist between Bitcoin and alternative cryptocurrencies.

It is necessary to have a firm grasp of the origins of Bitcoin and alternative cryptocurrencies in order to have any chance of understanding the distinctions between them. The first decentralized, peer-to-peer, blockchain- based digital currency was Bitcoin, which served as the model for subsequent cryptocurrencies. Its primary objective was to make it easier for users to conduct trustless transactions, hence removing the necessity for third parties in the value exchange process. In the years that followed, the rapidly expanding community surrounding cryptocurrencies came to the realization that blockchain technology had applications beyond those of a digital currency alone. This insight led to the conception of altcoins, which are alternative cryptocurrencies that are based on the principles of Bitcoin but extend their functionality in a variety of different directions.

The goals of each alternative cryptocurrency and the use cases they were designed for are one of the most significant differences between Bitcoin and other cryptocurrencies. Alternative cryptocurrencies, in contrast to Bitcoin, which is used primarily as a medium of exchange and a store of value, are frequently designed with a particular market or sector in mind. Ethereum, for example, was the first cryptocurrency to implement the notion of smart contracts and decentralized applications (DApps), both of which make it possible for developers to create complicated programs that run on Ethereum's blockchain. Because of this, Ethereum has been evolved into a platform that can host multiple blockchain-based applications beyond simple financial transactions. Ripple (XRP) came into being with the intention of reinventing international financial transactions and attempting to increase the effectiveness as well as the speed of internationally financial transactions. Cardano (ADA) places a high priority on research-driven development and has the goal of developing a blockchain platform that is both scalable and sustainable for a wide variety of uses. These examples illustrate how alternative cryptocurrencies have contributed to the diversification of the cryptocurrency ecosystem by alleviating certain problems and meeting a wide variety of requirements.

Bitcoin and other cryptocurrencies are distinguished from one another by underlying technological differences. Proof-of-work (PoW) is the name given to the consensus process that underpins Bitcoin's underlying technology, which is also known as blockchain. Miners compete with one another to solve difficult mathematical problems in order to validate transactions and create new blocks. On the other side, altcoins have experimented with a variety of other consensus mechanism. Ethereum, for instance, is in the process of transitioning from PoW to proof-of-stake (PoS), a mechanism that relies on validators who "stake" their coins to secure the network and validate transactions. This change is being made with the intention of enhancing scalability as well as energy efficiency. This will help solve some of the concerns that have been connected with Bitcoin's energy-intensive PoW.

A unique place in the market has been reserved for Bitcoin as a result of the fact that it was the first cryptocurrency and that it is so widely recognized. Bitcoin, which is also known as "digital gold," is viewed as a store of value and a hedge against economic risks, much like precious metals. This notion is one of the factors that has contributed to its comparatively low volatility in comparison to that of many alternative cryptocurrencies. The prices of altcoins, particularly those with lower market capitalizations, have a tendency to be more volatile as a result of variables like as lesser liquidity, swings in market sentiment, and their varying degrees of adoption and recognition.

The regulatory stances taken toward Bitcoin and other cryptocurrencies might vary greatly from one another. Because of its fame, Bitcoin has been subjected to increased regulatory scrutiny and recognition in a number of different jurisdictions. Regulatory responses to alternative cryptocurrencies can vary widely, depending on both the characteristics of the cryptocurrencies and the uses to which they are put. Alternative cryptocurrencies are regarded as digital assets by some nations, making them subject to specific rules; other governments may view them as securities or commodities. These regulatory nuances further highlight the need of differentiating between Bitcoin and altcoins, as they may be subject to different legal frameworks.

A culture of innovation and experimentation has been created inside the cryptocurrency industry as a result of the growth of alternative cryptocurrencies. The potential applications of blockchain technology continue to expand, and as a result, altcoin projects are always working to overcome the constraints that are currently in place. This experimentation has led to the introduction of tokens with distinct characteristics, such as coins with a focus on privacy, such as Monero (XMR) and Zcash (ZEC), stablecoins tied to real-world assets, such as the US Dollar Tether (USDT), and utility tokens built for specific roles inside decentralized ecosystems.

In conclusion, the differences between Bitcoin and alternative cryptocurrencies go well beyond a simple matter of terminology. The philosophies, use cases, and technological techniques that are embodied by these digital assets are each unique. While Bitcoin's legacy as the first cryptocurrency is indisputable, altcoins have emerged as a dynamic force, driving innovation, expanding utility, and redefining the boundaries of what blockchain technology can achieve. To successfully explore the complex world of cryptocurrencies, one has to have a solid understanding of the nuances that differentiate Bitcoin and altcoins from one another, as well as an appreciation for the numerous prospects that these cryptocurrencies bring for influencing the future of finance and technology.

Categories of Altcoins: Tokens, Platforms, Privacy Coins, and more

The landscape of cryptocurrencies is constantly shifting, and the word "altcoins" has come to refer to a wide array of cryptocurrencies and other digital assets that exist outside of the scope of Bitcoin. These alternative cryptocurrencies reflect a dynamic tapestry of innovation, with each one being tailored to address specific difficulties, industries, or consumer preferences in its own unique way. It is vital, in order to have a complete understanding of the enormous spectrum of cryptocurrencies, to delve into the categories that characterize them. These categories provide a view into the many facets that make up the cryptocurrency ecosystem, from privacy-focused alternatives and stablecoins to utility tokens and platform coins.

Utility tokens are likely to be one of the most well-known kinds of alternative cryptocurrencies. These tokens act as the fuel that keeps decentralized applications (DApps) and ecosystems running, and they give users access to particular functions or services that are included within a blockchain-based platform. Ether, the native currency of Ethereum, or ETH for short, is a great illustration of a utility token. On the Ethereum network, transactions and the deployment of smart contracts both require ETH as a fuel source. In a similar manner, Binance Coin (BNB) was first introduced on the Binance exchange as a utility token with the purpose of providing users with savings on trading fees and opportunities to participate in token sales held on the site. Utility tokens highlight the practical aspects of blockchain technology and make it possible for users to interact with decentralized applications (DApps) and ecosystems in a smooth manner.

Platform coins, also known as platform altcoins, are digital currencies that serve as the basis upon which decentralized applications (DApps), smart contracts, and other types of decentralized services can be constructed. As was discussed before, Ethereum stands out as the pioneering cryptocurrency in this area. Its blockchain offers developers a strong foundation on which they may build a wide variety of applications that go beyond simple financial transactions. EOS and Tron are two further examples of platform coins. Both of these cryptocurrencies provide developers with the tools and infrastructure necessary to construct decentralized applications that have certain capabilities and features. These platform currencies play a significant part in fostering innovation and expanding the value of blockchain technology beyond its initial use case as a currency. In other words, its primary function is to broaden the scope of blockchain technology's applications.

Individuals who are looking for increased anonymity and security in their financial dealings are the target market for privacy coins. Privacy coins, in contrast to Bitcoin transactions, which are pseudonymous and can be linked to specific addresses, make use of more advanced cryptographic algorithms to conceal transaction details, thereby giving users with increased levels of privacy. Monero (XMR) is a prominent cryptocurrency that prioritizes user privacy by employing ring signatures and stealth addresses in order to make transactions impossible to trace. Zcash (ZEC), another cryptocurrency, enables users to send and receive monetary transactions while maintaining a higher level of anonymity through the use of "shielded" transactions. Privacy coins offer an alternative to cryptocurrencies that place a priority on openness and solve the problem of maintaining the confidentiality of financial transactions.

There is a new subset of alternative cryptocurrencies known as stablecoins, and their primary objective is to reduce the price volatility that is common among cryptocurrencies. These digital assets are linked to assets that exist in the real world, such as fiat currencies that include the US Dollar or commodities such as gold. Users are able to transact and store funds with stablecoins without being subject to the price volatility that is typical of other cryptocurrencies. This bridge is provided by stablecoins, which provide a connection between the traditional financial system and the cryptocurrency realm. Stablecoins such as Tether (USDT), USD Coin (USDC), and DAI are some examples of cryptocurrencies that provide price stability while keeping the advantages of blockchain technology.

Governance tokens empower participants within a decentralized ecosystem to have a say in decision-making processes related to protocol upgrades, parameter changes, and the allocation of resources. Token holders have the capability to propose and vote on changes to a project's governance that could significantly affect the project's future. One prominent illustration of this type of token is MakerDAO's governance token, known as MKR. Holders of this token have the ability to take part in the management of the decentralized stablecoin known as DAI. Governance tokens are digital assets that allow stakeholders to have an active role in a project's direction and development by incorporating democratic and decentralized governance concepts into their design.

Interoperability coins are an attempt to solve the problem of insufficient connectivity across various blockchain networks. Their goal is to make communication and the exchange of value between multiple blockchains as smooth as possible, with the end goal of fostering collaboration and synergy within the decentralized ecosystem. One noteworthy example is Polkadot (DOT), which provides a multi-chain platform that enables many blockchains to interoperate with one another, share information, and trade value with one another. Interoperability coins are playing a critical part in the process of breaking down silos within the blockchain ecosystem. This makes it possible to design complex decentralized applications that can make use of the advantages provided by a variety of blockchain networks.

The plethora of alternative cryptocurrencies is a demonstration of the many facets that blockchain technology possesses as well as its potential to disrupt a variety of different markets. The subcategories of cryptocurrencies that have been discussed in this section, such as utility tokens, platform coins, privacy coins, stablecoins, governance tokens, and interoperability coins, only make up a small portion of the vast altcoin landscape. Each category performs a unique function, treating a particular kind of discomfort and pushing the limits of innovation in a new way. These altcoin categories will continue to play an important role in determining the course of the future of finance, technology, and decentralized applications even as the cryptocurrency ecosystem undergoes further change.

The Technological Innovations Driving Altcoin Development

In the fast-paced world of cryptocurrencies, innovation is the lifeblood that fuels progress and transformation. While Bitcoin laid the foundation for decentralized digital currencies, altcoins have taken the torch and run with it, pushing the boundaries of what blockchain technology can achieve. The development of altcoins is not a mere replication of Bitcoin's features; instead, it represents a quest to address its limitations, explore new functionalities, and redefine the possibilities within the digital landscape. The driving force behind the evolution of altcoins lies in the technological innovations that continue to shape their development.

One of the most significant technological leaps that altcoins have taken is the integration of smart contracts and decentralized applications (DApps). Ethereum, often hailed as the pioneer of this innovation, introduced the concept of programmable blockchain, enabling developers to create self-executing contracts and build intricate applications on its platform. This marked a departure from Bitcoin's primary focus on peer-to-peer transactions, expanding blockchain technology to encompass many real-world applications. Altcoins like Cardano (ADA) and Binance Smart Chain (BSC) further contribute to this trend by enhancing the capabilities of smart contracts, ensuring security, scalability, and interoperability.

As the popularity of cryptocurrencies grew, so did the challenge of scalability – the ability of a blockchain network to handle a high volume of transactions without compromising speed and efficiency. Bitcoin's block size limit and proof-of-work consensus mechanism led to congestion and slower transaction times during periods of high demand. Altcoins have responded with various scalability solutions. Ethereum, for instance, is working towards Ethereum 2.0, a major upgrade that will transition the network from proof-of-work to proof-of-stake and introduce sharding for enhanced scalability. Other altcoins, like Solana (SOL) and Avalanche (AVAX), implement novel consensus mechanisms and architectures to achieve higher throughput and lower latency, making them well-suited for decentralized finance (DeFi) applications.

While Bitcoin transactions are pseudonymous, meaning transaction details are public but linked to wallet addresses, altcoins have pioneered privacy-focused innovations to enhance transaction confidentiality. Privacy coins like Monero (XMR) and Zcash (ZEC) deploy advanced cryptographic techniques to obfuscate transaction details, ensuring that sender, receiver, and transaction amounts remain private. These technologies cater to users who prioritize anonymity and confidentiality in their transactions, a feature that Bitcoin struggles to provide due to its transparent ledger. Privacy-enhancing technologies address individual privacy concerns and lay the groundwork for the adoption of cryptocurrencies in industries that require confidentiality, such as healthcare and finance.

As the cryptocurrency landscape expands, seamless communication and value transfer between blockchains becomes increasingly crucial. Cross-chain interoperability solutions address this challenge by enabling tokens and data to flow between different blockchain networks. Altcoins like Polkadot (DOT) and Cosmos (ATOM) focus on creating interoperability platforms, allowing distinct blockchains to collaborate and share resources. These projects envision a future where blockchains no longer exist in isolation but function as an interconnected ecosystem, leveraging the strengths of various networks to create comprehensive solutions.

Bitcoin's energy-intensive proof-of-work (PoW) consensus mechanism has drawn criticism for its environmental impact. Altcoins are exploring alternatives that are more energy-efficient and environmentally friendly. Proof of stake, also known as PoS, is a consensus mechanism that is used by many alternative cryptocurrencies. In this system, validators are selected to create new blocks and keep the network secure based on the number of coins they "stake" as collateral. Ethereum's transition to Ethereum 2.0, including a shift to PoS, aims to reduce the network's energy consumption significantly. This focus on sustainability aligns with growing environmental awareness and demonstrates altcoins' commitment to adapting and evolving their technological foundations.

The development of altcoins is not a mere replication of Bitcoin's blueprint but an ongoing journey of technological exploration and innovation. Smart contracts, scalability solutions, privacy enhancements, cross-chain interoperability, and energy-efficient consensus mechanisms have driven altcoin development. These innovations address traditional financial systems' limitations and unlock new possibilities for industries across the spectrum. As altcoins continue to evolve, propelled by technological advancements, they paint a vivid picture of the transformative potential of blockchain technology, shaping a future where decentralized applications, secure transactions, and innovative solutions redefine how we interact with the digital world.

CHAPTER II

The Investment Potential of Altcoins

Historical Performance of Altcoins vs. Bitcoin

The world of cryptocurrencies has witnessed a transformative journey since the inception of Bitcoin in 2009. Bitcoin, often called digital gold, is the pioneer and benchmark for the entire cryptocurrency market. However, as the ecosystem expanded, it paved the way for many alternative cryptocurrencies, or altcoins, each with unique features and value propositions. A topic of considerable interest among investors and enthusiasts is the historical performance of altcoins compared to Bitcoin. Understanding the dynamics and trends that have shaped the relationship between these two categories of digital assets provides insights into the evolution of the cryptocurrency market.

In the nascent stages of the cryptocurrency market, Bitcoin reigned supreme. Its groundbreaking introduction of a decentralized digital currency captured the imagination of early adopters and tech enthusiasts. During these formative years, altcoins were few in number and often struggled to gain traction and recognition. Bitcoin's dominance in terms of market capitalization, trading volume, and overall recognition was virtually unchallenged.

As the cryptocurrency space matured, the emergence of altcoins brought new perspectives and possibilities. Ethereum's introduction of smart contracts in 2015 marked a pivotal moment, igniting a wave of innovation and diversification. Altcoins began experimenting with various functionalities like privacy features, scalability solutions, and specialized use cases. This diversification expanded the ecosystem and sparked debates about whether altcoins could surpass Bitcoin in terms of technological advancements and utility.

The cryptocurrency market is notorious for its volatility, with boom and bust cycles characterized by rapid price surges followed by steep corrections. Altcoins often experience these cycles, leading to the phenomenon known as "altcoin seasons." During altcoin seasons, the prices of various alternative cryptocurrencies can outpace Bitcoin's growth, attracting traders and investors seeking quick profits. However, during these times, there is a greater likelihood of market manipulation as well as an increase in the level of volatility.

Altcoins are more susceptible to fluctuations in market sentiment and hype-driven cycles. The crypto community's excitement surrounding a new project, technology, or use case can lead to substantial price spikes. Conversely, negative news or regulatory developments can trigger sharp price declines. As the foundational cryptocurrency, Bitcoin tends to be more resilient to short-term market sentiment shifts and external factors.

Bitcoin's unique position as the first cryptocurrency has given it a distinct role in the market. Bitcoin is frequently referred to as a "safe haven" asset, in the same vein as conventional safe-haven investments such as gold, particularly during times of economic uncertainty or global unrest. This perception has led to Bitcoin's adoption as a store of value, a digital equivalent to gold's role in preserving wealth. Altcoins, while innovative, have not achieved the same level of recognition and trust as Bitcoin in this context.

Several long-term trends emerge when examining the historical performance of altcoins vs. Bitcoin. Bitcoin's market dominance, measured by its share of the total cryptocurrency market capitalization, has experienced fluctuations over time. While altcoins have occasionally reduced Bitcoin's dominance during periods of heightened altcoin enthusiasm, Bitcoin consistently reasserts its dominance over the long term. This reflects Bitcoin's enduring status as the foundational cryptocurrency.

The success of Bitcoin and other cryptocurrencies in the past demonstrates how important it is for an investor's portfolio to be diversified and to have effective risk management. While altcoins can offer exciting opportunities for growth and innovation, they also come with increased volatility and higher risks. With its established history and recognition, Bitcoin often serves as a more stable foundation in a diversified portfolio, mitigating the potential impact of altcoin market fluctuations.

The historical performance of altcoins vs. Bitcoin paints a nuanced picture of the cryptocurrency market's evolution. Bitcoin's role as the pioneer and foundation has cemented its position as a digital store of value. On the other hand, Altcoins have showcased innovation, experimentation, and diverse use cases. While altcoins have at times experienced rapid price growth and market enthusiasm, Bitcoin's resilience and dominance underscore its enduring significance. Ultimately, the relationship between altcoins and Bitcoin is dynamic, shaped by technological advancements, market sentiment, and the pursuit of a decentralized future.

Diversification Benefits: Adding Altcoins to Your Portfolio

Investing in cryptocurrencies is a journey through uncharted territory, guided by the promise of innovation and the potential for substantial returns. At the forefront of this landscape is Bitcoin, the pioneer that introduced the world to the concept of decentralized digital currency. Yet, as the cryptocurrency ecosystem has evolved, many altcoins have emerged, each presenting unique features, use cases, and investment opportunities. The allure of altcoins lies in their potential for growth and in the diversification benefits they offer to investors seeking to navigate the complexities of this evolving market.

Diversification is a principle well-known in traditional finance, where spreading investments across different asset classes is used to manage risk and optimize returns. The market for cryptocurrencies operates according to the same concept. While Bitcoin remains a staple in many portfolios, the volatile nature of cryptocurrencies necessitates a strategic approach to risk mitigation. Altcoins, with their varied features and technologies, provide a means to diversify beyond the confines of Bitcoin, creating a well-rounded investment strategy that captures a broader range of opportunities.

One of the critical benefits of diversification through altcoins is the potential to mitigate risk associated with volatility and market fluctuations. Altcoins do not always move in lockstep with Bitcoin's price movements; they often have different correlation patterns. This means that while Bitcoin's price might experience a decline, certain altcoins could maintain their value or even appreciate it. By holding a mix of assets with diverse correlation profiles, investors can soften the impact of extreme market swings, enhancing the stability of their portfolio.

Altcoins represent a conduit for investors to gain exposure to technological innovations beyond the capabilities of Bitcoin. While Bitcoin's primary utility lies in being a decentralized digital currency, altcoins delve into many applications. Ethereum introduced smart contracts and decentralized applications, while other altcoins specialize in privacy, interoperability, and scalability solutions. By adding carefully selected altcoins to their portfolios, investors position themselves to capitalize on blockchain technology's ongoing progress and evolution.

The diversity of altcoins allows investors to target specific niches and emerging trends within the cryptocurrency space. For instance, decentralized finance (DeFi) has emerged as a prominent trend, offering decentralized alternatives to traditional financial services. Altcoins associated with DeFi platforms can provide exposure to this burgeoning sector, potentially reaping the rewards of its growth. Similarly, non-fungible tokens (NFTs) have gained immense traction, enabling ownership of unique digital assets. Altcoins linked to NFT platforms offer a gateway to this innovative realm, allowing investors to participate in the digital ownership revolution.

Diversification through altcoins requires a strategic approach to portfolio allocation. Investors must consider risk tolerance, investment goals, and time horizon. A well-diversified portfolio might include a blend of Bitcoin as a foundational asset and carefully selected altcoins that align with the investor's interests and objectives. It is absolutely necessary to carry out extensive research and exercise due diligence in order to evaluate the viability, team, technology, and prospective market demand of any alternative coin that is being considered.

While diversifying into altcoins presents compelling benefits, it's not without challenges. The altcoin landscape is vast and diverse, ranging from established projects with solid track records to speculative ventures with uncertain futures. Investors must exercise caution to avoid falling prey to scams, fraudulent schemes, and overly ambitious promises. Additionally, altcoins tend to exhibit higher volatility than Bitcoin, demanding a disciplined approach to risk management.

The evolution of the cryptocurrency market has ushered in an era of diversity and innovation, with altcoins playing a pivotal role in shaping its landscape. Diversification benefits extend beyond traditional finance, enabling investors to manage risk, gain exposure to emerging technologies, and capture opportunities in niche markets. Including altcoins in an investment portfolio requires thoughtful consideration, research, and a clear understanding of one's investment goals. As the cryptocurrency ecosystem continues to mature, the potential for diversification through altcoins remains an avenue for investors to engage with the ever-changing world of decentralized digital assets.

Assessing Risk and Reward: Altcoins vs. Traditional Investments

The world of finance is a dynamic environment, full of possibilities and risks that interact with one another to form the basis of monetary outcomes. In recent years, the appearance of cryptocurrencies, more especially altcoins, has added a new dimension to this scene. As a result, it has captured the interest of investors who are looking for novel paths through which potential growth can be achieved. As the popularity of altcoins continues to rise, it is more important than ever to conduct an in-depth analysis of the risk-to-reward ratio that these investments present in comparison to more conventional ones. To successfully traverse this difficult decision-making process, it is essential to have a solid understanding of the distinctive characteristics that characterize alternative cryptocurrencies and how these cryptocurrencies compare to more traditional investment options.

The term "alternative coins," which is shortened to "altcoins," refers to a wide variety of digital assets that exist beyond the domain of Bitcoin. They do this by utilizing blockchain technology, which allows them to create novel features, use cases, and capabilities. Altcoins strive to transform sectors beyond the boundaries of existing financial systems by providing features such as decentralized applications (DApps), smart contracts, solutions for protecting users' privacy, and interoperability. Investors that see the potential for exponential development and transformation in the cryptocurrency market are likely to find this innovation-driven approach appealing.

When compared to the risk profile of traditional investments, the cryptocurrency market, and particularly altcoins, present a very different picture of the risk landscape. It is common knowledge that cryptocurrencies, especially altcoins, are notorious for the inherent volatility that they possess, which manifests itself as fast price movements. This volatility may be both an opportunity and a reason for alarm to those who observe it. Some alternative cryptocurrencies have seen spectacular gains in a short period of time, but at the same time, they have also seen significant losses. This increased volatility brings a higher degree of risk when compared to traditional investments, which often exhibit more consistent price trends due to the established value of the assets being invested in.

When assessing risk and reward, one crucial aspect is the market's maturity. Traditional investment markets, such as stocks, bonds, and real estate, have evolved over centuries, cultivating established regulations, institutions, and frameworks. In contrast, the cryptocurrency market, including altcoins, is relatively nascent and continues to navigate the complexities of regulatory scrutiny, technological evolution, and market sentiment. This lack of maturity introduces uncertainties and regulatory risks that investors must factor into their decision-making process.

Investing in altcoins can offer the allure of early adoption rewards and the potential to support groundbreaking technologies. Many investors are drawn to altcoins for their potential to provide a front-row seat to technological innovation that could disrupt industries and transform economies. However, this innovation potential is balanced by the inherent uncertainty of whether a particular altcoin will succeed in realizing its goals. Unlike traditional investments, where established business models and track records provide a basis for evaluation, altcoins often require a deeper understanding of technology, development teams, and market dynamics.

For investors, one of the most important factors to take into account is an asset's liquidity, which corresponds to the ease with which it may be bought or sold without having a substantial impact on its price. Traditional investment markets tend to offer higher liquidity, allowing investors to enter and exit positions with minimal impact on price. In contrast, some altcoin markets, particularly those with smaller market capitalizations, may exhibit lower liquidity, making it more challenging to execute trades without influencing the asset's price. Additionally, altcoin markets can be susceptible to market manipulation due to their relatively lower trading volumes.

Regulatory factors are pivotal in assessing the risk-reward trade-off of altcoins versus traditional investments. While conventional investments are subject to well-established regulatory frameworks that provide investor protection and transparency, the regulatory landscape for cryptocurrencies is evolving. The lack of uniform regulations across jurisdictions introduces risks related to legal compliance, potential regulation changes, and the risk of investments in projects that may later be subject to regulatory actions.

The allure of altcoins lies in the potential for substantial returns within a relatively short period. Some altcoins have recorded remarkable gains, outperforming many traditional assets. However, these high returns are often accompanied by heightened volatility and the risk of substantial losses. While generally offering more moderate returns, traditional investments often provide stability that aligns with long-term wealth preservation goals.

When comparing altcoins to traditional investments, it is necessary to have a comprehensive awareness of the nuances that are inherent to each environment in order to make an accurate risk and reward assessment. Altcoins allow investors to engage with cutting-edge technologies and innovative projects, with the potential for exponential growth. However, this potential is accompanied by higher volatility, regulatory uncertainties, and market immaturity. Traditional investments offer stability, regulatory protection, and well-established frameworks, albeit with potentially more moderate returns. As investors navigate the complex decision of allocating capital, striking a balance between risk and reward becomes paramount, ensuring that investment strategies align with individual risk tolerance, objectives, and time horizons.

Factors Influencing Altcoin Prices and Market Trends

The world of cryptocurrencies is a dynamic and ever-evolving ecosystem, one in which digital assets known as altcoins – alternative coins to Bitcoin – thrive on innovation, technology, and market sentiment. Alternative cryptocurrencies' prices are subject to dramatic swings, which present both possibilities and challenges for cryptocurrency investors and enthusiasts alike. It is absolutely necessary to have a solid understanding of the elements that affect altcoin pricing and market trends in order to successfully navigate this complex ecosystem and make well-informed judgments. The dynamics of altcoin pricing and the broader market trends are shaped by a myriad of causes. These forces range from technology improvements and market sentiment all the way to macroeconomic factors and regulatory events.

The sentiment of the market is a significant factor in determining the pricing of alternative cryptocurrencies. Exciting and encouraging news, as well as the revelation of new collaborations, technological advancements, or successful product launches, can create excitement and enthusiasm, which can lead to price increases. Similar to how negative news, security breaches, or regulatory crackdowns can cause panic selling and dramatic price falls, such events can also cause investors to lose trust in the market. The cryptocurrency market is frequently characterized by sentiment-driven cycles, which can result in considerable price swings. These cycles may be caused by a number of variables, including but not limited to hype as well as FOMO (fear of missing out). Nevertheless, the volatility that is caused by sentiment can put investors in a position where they are more likely to make impulsive decisions on the basis of short-term trends.

Prices of alternative cryptocurrencies are susceptible to being considerably influenced by the introduction of new technologies and developments in this sector. Investors looking for projects with a competitive edge may be interested in altcoins that bring unique features, address concerns with scalability, increase privacy, or motivate interoperability. For instance, Ethereum's launch of smart contracts marked a historic turning point in the development of the blockchain industry, which in turn sparked a surge of interest and investment in the platform. The advancement of technology and the reaching of significant development milestones both have the potential to increase investor confidence and contribute to the market's ability to sustainably appreciate prices.

Regulatory changes, regardless of whether they are favorable or unfavorable, have the potential to have a considerable impact on the values of alternative cryptocurrencies. Clarity in regulations and legislation that is favorable to investors and projects can build confidence in those parties, which can then lead to increasing adoption and price appreciation. On the other hand, regulatory ambiguity or negative conclusions can generate an atmosphere of fear and uncertainty, which can result to a decrease in prices. Because the growing regulatory landscape varies across jurisdictions, it is vital for investors to remain knowledgeable about the legal implications of investing in specific altcoins. This makes it important for investors to stay informed about the legal ramifications of investing in specific altcoins.

The ease with which an asset may be bought or sold without significantly altering its price is referred to as market liquidity. This is an important component in the dynamics of the price of alternative cryptocurrencies. The prices of assets that have a higher liquidity tend to be more stable, as these assets are less likely to experience significant price changes as a direct result of a single major transaction. The amount of a cryptocurrency that is exchanged in a certain time period is referred to as its trading volume. Trading volume may be used to get insight into market activity and investor interest. Inadequate levels of liquidity and trading volume can make a market more volatile and open to the possibility of being manipulated price-wise.

Adoption and actual-world use cases are primary factors that influence the value of alternative cryptocurrencies. It is more likely that alternative cryptocurrencies will garner continuous interest from investors if they have applications in the real world and achieve popularity in particular markets or fields. For instance, altcoins that enable efficient cross-border payments, support decentralized finance (DeFi) services, or enhance supply chain transparency may be able to capture a market demand that determines the price trajectory of those altcoins. Adoption measures, like as the number of active users and the growth of decentralized applications, provide insight into the value of an alternative cryptocurrency as well as the potential price appreciation of that cryptocurrency.

The total value of a cryptocurrency that is circulating in the market is known as the market capitalization of that cryptocurrency. Market capitalization is commonly used as an indicator of an altcoin's relative size and significance within the larger market. Investors are keeping a watchful eye on Bitcoin's dominance, which can be understood as the cryptocurrency's market capitalization expressed as a proportion of the whole market for cryptocurrencies. Alterations in Bitcoin's market share can be an indicator of changes in investor preferences between Bitcoin and alternative cryptocurrencies. A decline in Bitcoin's dominance could indicate a rise in interest in other altcoins, while a rise in Bitcoin's dominance could indicate a flight to safety.

The value of altcoins can also be affected by macroeconomic factors such as the state of the world economy, geopolitical events, and decisions made by central banks regarding monetary policy.

Cryptocurrencies are not isolated from traditional financial markets, and events that impact traditional assets can have ripple effects across the cryptocurrency space. For instance, economic unpredictability may encourage investors to purchase cryptocurrencies as a hedge against the volatility of traditional markets, which may result in an increase in the price of altcoins.

Alternative coin values may be affected through market manipulation, which is a process in which people or groups attempt to artificially influence prices for the purpose of gaining personal advantage. Unwary investors might sustain huge losses if they participate in pump-and-dump schemes, which include artificially inflating the price of an alternative cryptocurrency before dumping it. Additionally, the purchasing and selling activity of major holders, also known as "whales," who control huge amounts of an alternative cryptocurrency can affect market values. The cryptocurrency market is subject to manipulation due to its relatively reduced liquidity when compared to traditional markets.

The price dynamics of altcoins are influenced by a multifaceted interplay of factors, ranging from advancements in technology and market sentiment to regulatory developments and macroeconomic conditions. Investors and enthusiasts who are navigating the cryptocurrency ecosystem need to maintain vigilance and ensure that they are up to date on the many dynamics that affect market trends. Despite the fact that the volatility and frequent price changes in the altcoin sector bring both opportunities and risks, individuals are given the ability to make educated decisions and participate in the developing world of cryptocurrencies when they have a full awareness of the elements that influence the market.

CHAPTER III

Researching Altcoins

Fundamental Analysis: Evaluating the Technology, Use Case, and Team

In the ever-evolving landscape of cryptocurrencies, the allure of altcoins – alternative digital currencies to Bitcoin – is undeniable. Altcoins present investors with a diverse array of opportunities beyond the foundational cryptocurrency. However, navigating the vast and dynamic altcoin market requires more than speculation; it demands a thorough understanding of the underlying factors that drive value and growth. Fundamental analysis, a meticulous evaluation of the technology, use case, and team behind an altcoin, emerges as a crucial tool in the arsenal of the prudent altcoin investor.

The technology underpinning an altcoin is the bedrock upon which its entire value proposition rests. Unlike traditional assets, altcoins' value often derives from their innovative use of blockchain technology and the problems they aim to solve. The first step in fundamental analysis involves a comprehensive assessment of the altcoin's technical architecture, consensus mechanism, scalability solutions, security features, and interoperability capabilities. A robust and technologically sound altcoin is more likely to sustain its relevance and weather market volatility.

Beyond technology, an altcoin's practical application or use case is pivotal in its success. Altcoins that address real-world problems, enhance efficiency, or provide solutions in finance, supply chain, healthcare, and beyond attract more attention from investors and users alike. Understanding the altcoin's intended purpose, its potential to disrupt existing industries, and the market demand it seeks to fulfill is essential in determining its long-term viability.

Behind every successful altcoin is a dedicated and skilled development team. The team members' expertise, experience, and commitment are critical indicators of an altcoin's potential for success. A transparent and accessible team that communicates updates, addresses community concerns, and demonstrates a track record of delivering on promises inspires confidence in investors. Thorough research into the team's background, prior achievements, and reputation within the cryptocurrency community is a crucial aspect of fundamental analysis.

The strength of an altcoin's community and its level of adoption contribute significantly to its market value and growth potential. An engaged and active community demonstrates a genuine interest in the project and fosters network effects that attract more users, developers, and investors. Monitoring social media channels, online forums, and participation in community-driven initiatives can provide insights into the level of enthusiasm surrounding the altcoin.

Compliance with applicable rules is of the utmost importance for the development of an alternative cryptocurrency, as the regulatory environment surrounding cryptocurrencies is constantly shifting. An altcoin's willingness and ability to navigate regulatory challenges while adhering to legal requirements contribute to its long-term viability. Understanding the altcoin's approach to compliance, its engagement with regulators, and its adherence to anti-money laundering (AML) and know-your-customer (KYC) protocols is essential in assessing its risk profile.

Tokenomics refers to the economic model governing an altcoin's token supply, distribution, and utility. A well-designed tokenomics model aligns incentives, rewards network participants, and ensures a balanced distribution of tokens. Investors should examine factors such as the total supply, distribution strategy, inflation rate, and the mechanisms that underpin the token's value within the ecosystem. Tokenomics can influence price stability, scarcity, and long-term value appreciation.

The altcoin market is competitive, with numerous projects vying for attention and adoption. A thorough analysis should include an assessment of the altcoin's unique value proposition compared to existing and potential competitors. Understanding the altcoin's differentiation, its advantages over similar projects, and its potential to capture market share can inform investment decisions.

Transparency is a hallmark of reputable altcoin projects. Transparent projects provide clear information about their development roadmap, milestones, partnerships, and financials. Regular communication with the community through official channels demonstrates accountability and a commitment to the project's success. Investors should be cautious of projects lacking transparency or lacking comprehensive information.

In the dynamic and fast-paced world of altcoin investing, fundamental analysis emerges as a critical tool for identifying promising projects and navigating the risks associated with the market. Evaluating the technology, use case, team, community engagement, regulatory compliance, tokenomics, competitive landscape, and transparency allows investors to make informed decisions aligned with their risk tolerance and investment goals. While altcoin investing offers unique opportunities for growth and innovation, conducting thorough fundamental analysis remains essential in separating valuable projects from speculative ventures in the ever-evolving altcoin landscape.

Technical Analysis: Analyzing Price Charts and Patterns

In the field of cryptocurrency investing, which is characterized by a dynamic combination of innovation and volatility, altcoins present investors with a wide variety of opportunities that extend beyond the sphere of Bitcoin. As investors navigate this ever-changing world, they look for tools that can help them make educated decisions, lessen the impact of potential risks, and spot emerging trends. Enter the field of technical analysis, which is a discipline that forecasts future price movements by analyzing past price data, chart patterns, and market indicators. For traders and investors alike, having the ability to understand and make use of technical analysis may be a very useful skill in the context of altcoin investing, where price volatility is an ever- present factor.

The basic principle of technical analysis is the notion that analyses of previous price data can reveal patterns that can be used to forecast future price movements. Analysts attempt to determine the sentiment of the market, recognize emerging trends, and come to judgments that are well-informed by analyzing price charts, patterns, and a variety of technical indicators. Technical analysis, on the other hand, is concerned with how market players perceive an asset's worth, in contrast to fundamental analysis, which focuses on the underlying reasons that drive an asset's value.

The canvas on which technical analysis is performed are price charts. The identification of trends is the key focus, and these trends can be broken down into three categories: uptrends, downtrends, and sideways trends (also known as consolidations). The market's sentiment, buying and selling pressure, and potential breakout or breakdown points can all be seen in detail on altcoin price charts. Chart patterns like as head and shoulders, triangles, and flags offer visual indicators that might assist in the process of predicting future price movements.

In technical analysis, the notions of support and resistance levels are extremely important. The price levels known as "support" are those at which an asset is likely to attract purchasing interest and halt any further drop. On the other hand, resistance refers to price levels that are met with increased selling interest and prevent any attempt at an upward movement. By locating these levels on charts of altcoin prices, investors may better anticipate the possibility of price reversals and make more educated judgments regarding whether to enter or exit the market.

In the field of technical analysis, moving averages are frequently applied in order to smooth out price data and discover trends. The simple moving averages (SMA) and the exponential moving averages (EMA) are two types of moving averages that can assist traders in filtering out short-term price changes and concentrating on longer-term trends. In addition, trend indicators such as the

Moving Average Convergence Divergence (MACD) and the Average Directional Index (ADX) provide traders with insights into the strength and direction of a trend, which helps traders analyze potential entry and exit positions in the market.

Oscillators and momentum indicators are pieces of technical analysis software that help traders determine the rate and magnitude of market fluctuations. For instance, the Stochastic Oscillator and Relative Strength Index (RSI) and measure overbought and oversold circumstances, which signal to probable reversal points in the market. Investors are able to determine whether the price of an altcoin may be about to undergo a correction or a trend reversal with the assistance of these indicators.

Patterns on a chart, such as triangles, rectangles, and wedges, might provide valuable information regarding the possible direction of prices in the future. Breakouts take place when the price of an alternative cryptocurrency breaks through a major support or resistance level. This signifies a shift in market sentiment and the possibility of an increase in price. Traders and investors who are familiar with chart patterns and who monitor breakout points are in a better position to profit on price momentum when opportunities arise.

Although it is a useful tool, technical analysis comes with a number of restrictions and possible risks. One obstacle is that looking at historical data and patterns of prices does not guarantee any particular outcome in the future. The emotion of the market might change suddenly as a result of unanticipated occurrences, rendering the predictions of technical analysis useless. Additionally, in comparison to traditional markets, the cryptocurrency market has a very low level of liquidity, which can result in heightened price volatility and manipulation. This has an effect on the usefulness of technical analysis tools.

Combining fundamental and technical analysis is a crucial component of a well-rounded strategy for investing in alternative cryptocurrencies. Fundamental analysis investigates a cryptocurrency's core technology, development team, and market potential, in contrast to technical analysis, which focuses on price patterns and indicators. The combination of these two methodologies can provide a more thorough view of the possibilities of an alternative coin, thereby assisting investors in making decisions that are well-informed.

In the area of investing in alternative cryptocurrencies, where price volatility is an ever-present companion, technical analysis provides a roadmap to successfully navigate the complex market dynamics. Technical analysts attempt to identify trends, reversals, and potential breakout points through the analysis of price charts, patterns, indicators, and oscillators. Nevertheless, it is absolutely necessary to realize the constraints and risks involved with technical analysis, such as the possibility that unanticipated occurrences will break patterns that have been expected. Investors can leverage the power of technical analysis to make educated judgments in the world of altcoin investing by integrating technical analysis with other analytical approaches and realizing that no tool can anticipate market behavior with certainty. By doing so, investors will be able to keep up with the ever-changing world of altcoin investment.

Market Sentiment and News Analysis: Gauging Community and Media Influence

The world of cryptocurrency investing is a realm where innovation and volatility intertwine, giving rise to a landscape that is as dynamic as it is challenging. Amid this volatility, altcoins – alternative digital currencies to Bitcoin – offer unique opportunities for investors seeking diversification and potential growth. Market sentiment and news analysis are crucial in shaping price movements and investor decisions in this landscape. Understanding the influence of community sentiment and media coverage on altcoin investing is paramount for those navigating the intricate web of cryptocurrency markets.

Market sentiment, often called the collective mood of market participants, is a potent force driving price movements in cryptocurrency. The unique nature of altcoins and the absence of traditional valuation metrics place significant importance on sentiment as a determinant of price trends. Positive sentiment, driven by excitement about new technologies, partnerships, or use cases, can lead to price surges. Conversely, negative sentiment from security breaches, regulatory concerns, or other adverse events can result in sharp price declines.

In the world of altcoins, community engagement is a driving force that can shape market sentiment. Altcoin communities, often comprising developers, enthusiasts, and investors, actively share information, discuss projects, and advocate for specific assets. Positive or negative sentiment within these communities can have a cascading effect on broader market sentiment. For instance, a solid and engaged community can amplify positive news and fuel upward price momentum, while a divided or disillusioned community can contribute to price stagnation or declines.

Social media and online forums are virtual gathering places for cryptocurrency enthusiasts, investors, and stakeholders. These platforms provide a space for sharing news, discussing trends, and expressing opinions. The sentiments expressed on platforms like Twitter, Reddit, and Telegram can serve as barometers for the broader market sentiment. Monitoring these platforms can provide insights into emerging trends, potential opportunities, and market sentiment shifts.

Influencers, individuals with a significant online following and expertise in cryptocurrency, can sway market sentiment through their analyses, opinions, and endorsements. Their followers often look to them for insights and guidance, making their statements capable of sparking price movements. However, the impact of influencers comes with a caveat: their recommendations can sometimes be divisive, and investors should exercise caution and perform extensive research before making judgments that are purely based on the opinions of influencers.

Media coverage, both mainstream and within the cryptocurrency industry, significantly shapes market sentiment. Positive news coverage can highlight technological advancements, adoption milestones, and industry developments, boosting investor confidence and fueling positive sentiment. On the other hand, negative news that include a breach in security or regulatory crackdowns can cause panic selling and decrease sentiment in the market. Investors must critically assess news sources' credibility and consider news events' potential impact on altcoin prices.

Market sentiment and news analysis can trigger a cascading effect, magnifying price movements. Positive news can lead to FOMO (fear of missing out), prompting investors to buy, further increasing prices. Similarly, negative news can incite panic selling, causing prices to plummet. These rapid shifts in sentiment and corresponding price movements can create opportunities for traders and investors, but they also demand a clear understanding of the market dynamics and the ability to react swiftly.

While community sentiment and media coverage can provide valuable insights, they are not immune to misinformation and manipulation. False or exaggerated claims, rumors, and coordinated efforts to spread misinformation can lead to rapid shifts in sentiment that do not accurately reflect the underlying fundamentals of altcoins. Investors should exercise caution, verify information from credible sources, and approach news analysis with a critical mindset.

Investing in altcoins requires navigating sentiment-driven markets where news events, social media discussions, and community sentiment can significantly impact prices. Investors must balance capitalizing on sentiment-driven opportunities and ensuring that a combination informs their decisions of technical analysis, fundamental analysis, and a deep understanding of the altcoin's technology, use case, and team. By adopting a multidimensional approach to altcoin investing, investors can mitigate the risks associated with sentiment-driven price fluctuations.

In the intricate world of altcoin investing, market sentiment and news analysis hold the power to shape price trends and investor decisions. Understanding the influence of community sentiment, social media platforms, influencers, and media coverage is essential for navigating the volatile cryptocurrency landscape. While sentiment-driven markets offer opportunities for swift gains, they also demand a cautious and well-informed approach. Investors can harness the power of market sentiment while making informed decisions that are in line with their risk tolerance and investment goals if they combine sentiment analysis with other analytical tools and do extensive research.

Identifying Red Flags: Avoiding Scams and Shady Projects

Cryptocurrency investing offers a landscape of innovation, potential gains, and opportunities. However, within this realm lurk risks and threats that demand a discerning eye and cautious approach. Altcoins, alternative digital currencies to Bitcoin, present a diverse range of projects and investments, but they also attract malicious actors looking to exploit unsuspecting investors. Identifying red flags and avoiding scams and shady projects is paramount for those seeking to navigate the altcoin market safely and profitably.

Transparency is a hallmark of legitimate and credible projects in the cryptocurrency space. Shady projects often lack transparency in various aspects, including the identity of the development team, project goals, technical documentation, and financial information. A lack of transparency makes it difficult for investors to assess the legitimacy and viability of an altcoin, raising suspicions about the project's intentions.

Shady projects often make exaggerated claims and promises that are too good to be true. Promises of guaranteed high returns, instant wealth, or groundbreaking technological advancements should raise caution. Investment decisions based on unrealistic promises can lead to significant financial losses. Altcoin investors should approach projects that rely solely on hype and promises with skepticism and conduct thorough research before committing funds.

Legitimate altcoin projects are driven by a clear use case and innovative technology that solves real-world problems. Shady projects may lack a clear value proposition or offer vague purpose descriptions. Investors should be wary of altcoins that fail to articulate a practical use case or technical innovations that differentiate them from other projects.

Whitepapers serve as the foundational documents outlining an altcoin project's technology, purpose, and mechanics. Shady projects may lack comprehensive whitepapers or offer poorly written, plagiarized, or incomprehensible documents. Additionally, they may provide limited technical details or refuse to share the inner workings of their technology. Investors should prioritize projects that provide well-documented whitepapers and technical explanations.

While token sales and fundraising are legitimate methods of financing altcoin projects, an overemphasis on fundraising without a clear product development and adoption plan can be a red flag. Shady projects may prioritize token sales over delivering a viable product or solution, leaving investors with worthless tokens and dashed expectations.

Shady projects often rely on unverified claims and endorsements to gain credibility. These claims may involve partnerships with well-known companies, celebrity endorsements, or participation in prestigious events. Investors should verify such claims independently and be cautious of projects that rely solely on endorsements to attract attention.

Legitimate altcoin projects foster active and engaged communities that discuss, critique, and support the project's development. Shady projects may lack genuine community engagement or resort to fake social media accounts and paid followers to create the illusion of popularity. Investors should assess the authenticity of a project's community engagement and interactions.

Shady projects often employ high-pressure tactics to encourage investors to make hasty investment decisions. Tactics such as limited-time offers, fear of missing out (FOMO), and urgency to invest before a specific deadline are signs of potential scams. Investors should take their time to conduct thorough due diligence and should be cautious of projects that rush them into making investment decisions.

Compliance with regulatory requirements is a hallmark of legitimate projects in the cryptocurrency space. Shady projects may lack proper registration, licensing, or adherence to legal frameworks. Investors should prioritize projects that demonstrate compliance with relevant regulations and guidelines to ensure the safety of their investments.

The credibility and experience of the development team are crucial in assessing the legitimacy of an altcoin project. Shady projects may provide insufficient or unverifiable information about their team members' backgrounds and expertise. Investors should thoroughly research the project's development team, their previous projects, and their reputation within the cryptocurrency community.

As the altcoin market continues to expand, the importance of identifying red flags and avoiding scams cannot be overstated. Shady projects and malicious actors seek to capitalize on investors' enthusiasm and lack of awareness. A cautious and diligent approach, driven by thorough research, critical thinking, and skepticism, is essential for responsibly safeguarding investments and participating in the altcoin market. By staying informed, conducting due diligence, and being vigilant about red flags, investors can confidently navigate the altcoin landscape and reduce the risk of falling victim to scams and shady projects.

CHAPTER IV

Prominent Altcoins in the Market

Ethereum (ETH): The Smart Contract Pioneer

In the realm of cryptocurrencies, few projects have captured the imagination and innovation of the world quite like Ethereum (ETH). Often hailed as more than a digital currency, Ethereum has revolutionized how we think about blockchain technology and its potential applications. As the second-largest cryptocurrency by market capitalization, Ethereum's significance extends beyond its market value – it lies at the heart of a decentralized ecosystem that has given rise to decentralized applications (DApps), decentralized finance (DeFi), and the concept of smart contracts. In this section, we delve into the origins, features, and impact of Ethereum, exploring how it has paved the way for a new era of blockchain-based possibilities.

Vitalik Buterin conceptualized Ethereum in late 2013, with the whitepaper published in 2013. Ethereum was developed with the intention of providing a decentralized platform for the development of applications and the execution of smart contracts, in contrast to Bitcoin, which was initially conceived as a digital currency and payment system. Launched in July 2015, Ethereum's genesis block marked the beginning of a new era, enabling developers to create and deploy decentralized applications that could revolutionize industries beyond finance.

At the core of Ethereum's innovation lies the concept of smart contracts. Smart contracts are agreements that can carry out their terms automatically and have those terms inscribed straight into computer code. They run by themselves without the need for any intermediaries whenever the requirements that have been set are satisfied. This feature opens up a world of possibilities across various industries, from supply chain management and real estate to gaming and digital identity verification. The introduction of smart contracts has transformed how business agreements are conceptualized and executed, significantly reducing the need for intermediaries and streamlining processes.

The Ethereum Virtual Machine (EVM) is the decentralized computing environment that executes smart contracts. It enables developers to write code in multiple programming languages and deploy it on the Ethereum blockchain. This versatility has contributed to Ethereum's popularity, as developers with diverse programming backgrounds can contribute to the ecosystem. The widespread adoption of Ethereum-compatible programming languages like Solidity has enabled a thriving developer community to create innovative DApps and smart contracts.

Ethereum's smart contract capabilities laid the foundation for the proliferation of decentralized applications (DApps). These applications operate on the Ethereum blockchain, offering users a decentralized and transparent alternative to traditional platforms. Furthermore, Ethereum's impact on finance cannot be overstated. The rise of decentralized finance (DeFi) platforms built on Ethereum has unlocked new avenues for borrowing, lending, trading, and yield farming without intermediaries. DeFi's rapid growth has drawn attention to the power of blockchain technology in redefining traditional financial services.

While Ethereum has achieved remarkable milestones, it has also faced challenges concerning scalability and energy efficiency. Ethereum's move to Ethereum 2.0, also known as Eth2 or Serenity, addresses these concerns by transitioning from a proof-of-work (PoW) consensus mechanism to a proof-of-stake (PoS) mechanism. This upgrade is expected to improve transaction speed, reduce energy consumption, and enable greater scalability, positioning Ethereum for a more sustainable and efficient future.

Despite its groundbreaking achievements, Ethereum has its challenges. Scalability issues, high gas fees during periods of network congestion, and interoperability hurdles have prompted the development of alternative blockchain platforms aiming to address these limitations. Competitors like Binance Smart Chain, Solana, and Polkadot offer different approaches to solving blockchain's scalability problem and pose as potential alternatives to Ethereum for developers and users.

Ethereum's impact on the broader cryptocurrency landscape is undeniable. It pioneered the idea of smart contracts and offered a forum for programmers to bring their blockchain-based concepts to life. The surge in ICOs (Initial Coin Offerings) during the initial coin offering boom was primarily powered by Ethereum's platform. Additionally, Ethereum's success paved the way for the emergence of thousands of tokens and altcoins, contributing to the vibrant and diverse cryptocurrency market we see today.

As Ethereum continues to evolve, ethical considerations come to the forefront. The rise of DeFi platforms has brought attention to regulatory and security challenges. Smart contracts, while powerful, are not immune to bugs or vulnerabilities, leading to potential risks for users and investors. As Ethereum progresses toward Ethereum 2.0, it will be interesting to observe how the network addresses these concerns while maintaining its position as a pioneering force in blockchain.

The path that was taken by Ethereum to go from a whitepaper to a worldwide sensation is illustrative of the power of innovation and vision. Its introduction of smart contracts and the Ethereum Virtual Machine has forever changed how we approach agreements, transactions, and decentralized applications. Ethereum's impact extends beyond technology, inspiring developers, entrepreneurs, and enthusiasts to explore the potential of blockchain in reshaping industries. Ethereum remains a guiding light, illuminating the route toward a future that is more decentralized, efficient, and equitable as the blockchain ecosystem continues to develop and deal with difficulties.

Ripple (XRP): Transforming Cross-Border Payments

In the dynamic landscape of cryptocurrencies, Ripple (XRP) stands out as a project with a distinct focus on transforming the way cross-border payments are conducted. While many cryptocurrencies strive to serve as digital currencies or store of value, Ripple has taken a unique approach by targeting the inefficiencies and challenges that persist within the global remittance and payments industry. With a vision to provide faster, more efficient, and cost-effective cross-border transactions, Ripple has positioned itself as a trailblazer in financial technology. In this section, we explore the origins, features, and impact of Ripple (XRP) as a catalyst for change in the cross-border payments ecosystem.

Ripple's journey began in 2012 when Jed McCaleb and Chris Larsen co-founded OpenCoin, the company that later developed the Ripple protocol. Originally named OpenCoin, the project was rebranded as Ripple Labs in 2013, and the cryptocurrency associated with the protocol was called XRP. Ripple's primary focus was to address the inefficiencies and high costs associated with cross-border payments, a challenge that has plagued the traditional banking system for years.

At the heart of Ripple's innovation lies the Ripple protocol, which facilitates the seamless transfer of value between parties. Unlike many other cryptocurrencies, XRP is not designed to be a digital currency for general transactions but serves as a bridge currency within the Ripple network. The Ripple protocol allows for the real-time transfer of various assets, including fiat currencies and commodities, across borders without intermediaries or traditional banking processes.

Ripple's transformative impact is primarily attributed to its RippleNet network. RippleNet is an international community of banks, financial institutions, as well as payment service providers that use Ripple's technology to conduct cross-border payments. Through RippleNet, participants can settle transactions in seconds, eliminating the delays and uncertainties often accompanying traditional international transfers. This speed and efficiency could revolutionize how money moves across borders.

Ripple employs a consensus algorithm known as the Ripple Protocol Consensus Algorithm (RPCA), which differs from the proof-of-work (PoW) and proof-of-stake (PoS) mechanisms used by many other cryptocurrencies. The RPCA enables rapid transaction confirmation and consensus among network participants, contributing to the network's scalability and efficiency.

Ripple's impact on the cross-border payments industry is underscored by its partnerships and adoption by financial institutions. By collaborating with banks and payment providers worldwide, Ripple has demonstrated its commitment to reshaping the traditional financial system. Ripple's partnerships with institutions like Santander, American Express, and Standard Chartered have facilitated the integration of its technology into mainstream financial services, enhancing cross-border payment capabilities.

Remittances, or sending funds by individuals to their families in other countries, represent a critical aspect of the global economy. However, traditional remittance services' high fees and delays have led to financial exclusion and inefficiencies. Ripple aims to alleviate these challenges by offering a cost-effective and swift alternative for cross-border remittances, enabling individuals to send funds across borders with minimal fees and near-instant settlement times.

While Ripple's approach to cross-border payments is promising, it has faced its share of challenges. Regulatory concerns regarding the classification of XRP as security and ongoing legal battles with the U.S. Securities and Exchange Commission (SEC) have impacted the project's trajectory. The outcome of these legal proceedings has implications for Ripple and the broader cryptocurrency industry, as it could set precedents for how cryptocurrencies are regulated.

Ripple's impact on the cross-border payments industry is undeniable. Its technology has the potential to streamline international transactions, reduce costs, and enhance financial inclusion for individuals who rely on remittances. Ripple's role in defining the future of cross-border payments could become even more established as the regulatory landscape becomes clearer. Additionally, Ripple's expansion into new markets and partnerships with financial institutions will likely play a pivotal role in determining its future trajectory.

Ripple's journey from its inception to its current role as a transformative force in cross-border payments underscores the power of innovation and vision within cryptocurrency. By addressing the challenges of traditional cross-border transactions and leveraging blockchain technology, Ripple has positioned itself as a leader in driving efficiency and accessibility in the global remittance industry. As it navigates regulatory challenges and expands its network of partnerships, Ripple remains a symbol of how cryptocurrency technology can disrupt and enhance the financial landscape, making cross-border payments faster, more cost-effective, and more inclusive.

Cardano (ADA): A Third-Generation Blockchain Platform

Cardano (ADA) emerges as a prominent player in the rapidly evolving landscape of blockchain technology, distinguished by its commitment to scientific research, scalability, and sustainability. As a third-generation blockchain platform, Cardano aims to address the limitations of previous generations while offering a robust and versatile ecosystem for decentralized applications and smart contracts. With a meticulous focus on academic rigor and a commitment to technological innovation, Cardano seeks to usher in a new era of blockchain solutions. In this section, we delve into the origins, features, and impact of Cardano (ADA) as a pioneer in third-generation blockchain platforms.

Cardano's journey began with the vision of Charles Hoskinson, one of the co-founders of Ethereum. Founded in 2017, Cardano was designed to overcome the shortcomings of first-generation blockchains, such as Bitcoin, and second-generation blockchains, like Ethereum. Cardano's development is underpinned by a scientific and research-driven approach, seeking to combine the best features of existing blockchains while addressing their inherent limitations.

Cardano's unique approach to development is characterized by its commitment to scientific research and peer review. The platform is guided by a philosophy of research-driven design, where solutions are rigorously tested, peer-reviewed, and refined before implementation. This approach ensures that Cardano's technology is innovative and well-founded, enhancing its potential for real-world applications.

Cardano's architecture is divided into distinct layers, each serving a specific purpose. The settlement layer, which handles the ADA cryptocurrency, ensures the secure transfer of value. On the other hand, the computation layer is what makes it possible to carry out the execution of smart contracts and also decentralized applications. This separation of layers enhances scalability and modularity, allowing for upgrades and improvements without disrupting the entire ecosystem.

Cardano employs a unique proof-of-stake (PoS) protocol known as Ouroboros. Unlike traditional proof-of-work (PoW) consensus mechanisms, PoS is energy-efficient and addresses the environmental concerns associated with PoW-based blockchains. Ouroboros ensures secure and reliable transactions while allowing ADA holders to participate in the consensus process by staking their tokens.

Cardano strongly emphasizes scalability and interoperability, aiming to create a blockchain platform capable of handling a high volume of transactions without compromising performance. By using a layered architecture, sidechains, and protocols like RINA (Recursive InterNetwork Architecture), Cardano seeks to address the scalability challenges faced by earlier generations of blockchains.

Cardano's primary mission is to encourage the creation of decentralized applications (DApps) and smart contracts as part of its infrastructure. The Cardano platform allows developers to create and deploy secure and scalable smart contracts, enabling various applications in fields like finance, supply chain management, healthcare, and more. This opens the door for innovation while ensuring a robust and reliable environment for DApps to thrive.

Cardano's commitment to sustainability extends beyond technology to governance and environmental impact. The platform embraces a treasury system that allocates funds for development, maintenance, and improvements based on community proposals and voting. Cardano's proof-of-stake consensus mechanism also contributes to its energy efficiency and aligns with its focus on sustainability.

Cardano's research-driven approach and technological innovations have attracted collaborations with governments, enterprises, and academic institutions. The platform's focus on compliance, identity, and financial services has led to real-world applications, including partnerships in countries like Ethiopia and Georgia. These partnerships highlight Cardano's potential to drive socioeconomic change and empower underserved communities.

While Cardano's approach is lauded for its scientific rigor, it has also faced criticism for its systematic development timeline. Critics argue that the emphasis on research and peer review has led to delays in feature delivery. On the other hand, Cardano's long-term vision and commitment to quality place it in a position to continue its expansion and affect the blockchain industry.

Cardano's journey from concept to a third-generation blockchain platform is a testament to the power of academic rigor, research-driven design, and innovation. By addressing the limitations of previous blockchain generations and prioritizing scalability, sustainability, and interoperability, Cardano has positioned itself as a trailblazer in blockchain technology. As it continues to forge partnerships, launch applications, and refine its ecosystem, Cardano stands as a symbol of how blockchain's potential can be realized through meticulous planning, scientific inquiry, and a steadfast commitment to progress.

Solana (SOL): High-Performance Blockchain for DeFi

Solana (SOL) has emerged as a fascinating participant in the ever-evolving field of blockchain technology. They promise a high-performance and scalable platform for decentralized applications (DApps) and decentralized finance (DeFi). With its innovative approach to consensus, transaction speed, and scalability, Solana seeks to address the limitations that have hindered the growth and adoption of previous blockchain platforms. As the demand for DeFi solutions continues to rise, Solana's commitment to performance and efficiency positions it as a leading contender in reshaping the future of decentralized finance. In this section, we delve into the origins, features, and impact of Solana (SOL) as a high-performance blockchain platform tailored for DeFi applications.

Solana was founded by Anatoly Yakovenko in 2017 to overcome the scalability challenges existing blockchain platforms face. Drawing inspiration from his background in distributed systems and network protocols, Yakovenko aimed to create a blockchain that could deliver high throughput without sacrificing security or decentralization. Solana's approach to consensus and scalability differentiates it from its predecessors and places it at the forefront of blockchain innovation.

Solana introduces a unique consensus mechanism called Proof of History (PoH), which complements its primary consensus mechanism, Proof of Stake (PoS). PoH is a cryptographic clock that generates historical records of events in the blockchain. By providing a verifiable and timestamped order of events, PoH enhances the efficiency of consensus and enables nodes to agree on the order of transactions without constant communication. This innovation significantly improves scalability and transaction finality.

One of Solana's standout features is its exceptional transaction throughput. The combination of PoH and PoS allows Solana to process thousands of transactions per second, making it well-suited for applications with high-demand and fast-paced environments. The platform's performance is particularly beneficial for DeFi, where the speed and efficiency of transactions are critical for user experience.

Solana's architecture incorporates a unique form of sharding, a technique used to increase network scalability. In Solana's case, sharding is achieved through a multi-threaded approach, where different parts of the blockchain process transactions independently in parallel. This division of work enhances scalability and ensures the network can handle increased transaction volumes without compromising performance.

Solana's high-performance infrastructure is particularly appealing for DeFi applications. DeFi relies on quick and cost-effective transactions to facilitate lending, borrowing, trading, and yield farming activities. Solana's architecture enables DeFi protocols to operate efficiently and offer users a seamless experience. As the DeFi ecosystem expands, Solana's capabilities position it as a strong contender to support the growing demand.

Solana's focus on interoperability and cross-chain compatibility opens the door for seamless collaboration between different blockchain platforms. Through projects like Wormhole, Solana enables the transfer of assets and data between different blockchains. This capability enhances the broader blockchain ecosystem and contributes to the vision of a connected and interoperable decentralized future.

Solana's technology has attracted the attention of various projects, including decentralized exchanges, prediction markets, and gaming platforms. These applications leverage Solana's high throughput and low latency to enhance users' experiences. Partnerships with projects like Serum, Raydium, and Mango Markets showcase Solana's potential to drive innovation and adoption in the DeFi space.

While Solana has achieved significant milestones, it has challenges. As the platform gains attention and adoption, ensuring network security and decentralization becomes increasingly essential. Solana's approach to consensus and scalability may also raise questions about energy consumption and environmental impact, mainly as the platform grows in size and user base.

Solana's ascent from its inception to a high-performance blockchain platform is a testament to the power of innovation and determination within the blockchain space. Solana has positioned itself as a contender to drive the evolution of DeFi and decentralized applications by addressing scalability and transaction speed. As it navigates challenges and expands its ecosystem, Solana stands as a symbol of how blockchain technology can redefine the limits of what is possible, offering a high-performance foundation for a decentralized financial future.

Polkadot (DOT): Interoperability and Cross-Chain Compatibility

Polkadot (DOT) has established itself as a groundbreaking platform in the fast developing world of blockchain technology. This platform places a high priority on interoperability and cross-chain compatibility. As the blockchain ecosystem expands, the need for seamless collaboration between different blockchains has become increasingly apparent. Polkadot, founded by Ethereum co-founder Dr. Gavin Wood, seeks to address this obstacle by providing a framework that enables various blockchain networks to communicate and share information, unlocking new possibilities for innovation and collaboration. In this section, we delve into the origins, features, and impact of Polkadot (DOT) as a trailblazer in the realm of interoperable blockchain networks.

Polkadot's inception can be traced back to the vision of Dr. Gavin Wood, who co-founded Ethereum and played a crucial role in its development. With a deep understanding of the limitations of existing blockchains, Wood sought to create a platform that could overcome barriers to interoperability, scalability, and governance. The result was Polkadot, a project that aimed to address these challenges and introduced a novel approach to blockchain network interaction.

Polkadot's core innovation lies in its ability to connect multiple blockchains, enabling them to work together seamlessly as a unified network. This concept, known as interoperability, addresses one of the most pressing issues in the blockchain space – the fragmentation of various blockchain networks that operate in isolation. By providing a framework for blockchains to communicate and share information, Polkadot facilitates collaboration, data exchange, and the transfer of assets across different chains.

At the heart of Polkadot's interoperability is its Relay Chain, the leading blockchain that coordinates and validates transactions across the network. Parachains, on the other hand, are individual blockchains that connect to the Relay Chain and operate in parallel. These Parachains can be customized to suit specific use cases, allowing developers to create specialized blockchains for various applications while still benefiting from the security and consensus of the overall Polkadot network.

Polkadot's architecture enables cross-chain compatibility, seamlessly transferring assets between different blockchains. This feature has far-reaching implications, removing the need for intermediaries and centralized exchanges to facilitate asset swaps. Users can transact directly between different blockchains, unlocking liquidity and efficiency while reducing dependency on third-party services.

Polkadot's approach to scalability is rooted in its ability to connect multiple Parachains, each of which can process transactions independently. This parallel processing capability enhances the network's scalability and throughput, enabling it to handle more transactions than traditional single-chain blockchains. Additionally, Polkadot introduces a novel governance model that allows stakeholders to propose and vote on upgrades, changes, and improvements to the network, fostering a more decentralized decision-making process.

Polkadot's significance extends beyond its technical innovations; it also bridges the gap between different blockchain networks, creating a collaborative environment that encourages sharing ideas and solutions. Projects that build on Polkadot can leverage its interoperability features to access resources and functionalities from other blockchains, fostering an ecosystem of innovation and cross-pollination.

Polkadot's interoperability features profoundly impact the decentralized finance (DeFi) ecosystem. By enabling DeFi protocols to interoperate, Polkadot offers users a more seamless and connected experience, reducing fragmentation and improving overall efficiency. Beyond the realm of DeFi, Polkadot's capabilities include applications in a variety of domains, including management of supply chains, identity verification, gaming, and more.

While Polkadot's approach to interoperability and cross-chain compatibility is promising, it has challenges. Ensuring security, consensus, and proper coordination among Parachains is crucial to maintaining the integrity of the network. As Polkadot grows and attracts more projects, ensuring smooth communication and resource allocation among Parachains will be paramount.

Polkadot's journey from concept to a groundbreaking platform for interoperability and cross-chain compatibility is a testament to the power of innovation and collaboration within the blockchain space. Polkadot is redefining the possibilities of blockchain technology by addressing the limitations of isolated blockchains and fostering an environment of collaboration. As it continues to bridge the gap between different blockchains, Polkadot stands as a symbol of how interoperability can unlock new frontiers of innovation, connectivity, and efficiency in the ever-expanding world of blockchain networks.

CHAPTER V

Navigating the Altcoin Ecosystem

Wallets and Security: Safeguarding Your Altcoin Investments

In the realm of cryptocurrency investments, safeguarding your assets is of paramount importance. With the rise of altcoins and the increasing diversity of investment options, ensuring the security of your holdings has become more complex and crucial than ever. Securing your altcoin investments begins with choosing the right wallet and adopting best practices for safeguarding digital assets.

The significance of wallet security cannot be overstated. Cryptocurrency wallets serve as digital vaults for your digital assets, allowing you to securely store, send, and receive altcoins. Given the decentralized nature of cryptocurrencies, the responsibility for securing your investments rests squarely on your shoulders. The unique properties of cryptocurrencies, such as irreversible transactions and ownership via private keys, underscore the need for robust security measures.

Regarding wallets, several types are available, each with its security features and use cases. Hardware wallets, for instance, are physical devices that store your private keys offline. They offer high security by keeping your keys away from potential online threats. Hardware wallets are ideal for long-term storage and are relatively immune to malware and hacking attacks.

Software wallets, on the other hand, are applications that a user can download and install on their personal computer or mobile device. They are convenient for daily transactions but may be susceptible to malware or phishing attacks if your device is compromised. Meanwhile, web wallets are online platforms allowing you to access your altcoins from any device with an internet connection. While they offer convenience, they require you to trust a third party with your private keys, making them less secure.

Regardless of your wallet type, implementing best practices is essential to safeguard your altcoin investments. Use strong, unique passwords for your wallets to prevent unauthorized access. Enable Two-Factor Authentication (2FA) to add an extra layer of security. This requires a second verification form, such as a code delivered to your mobile device, before granting access to your wallet.

Regularly backing up your wallet's private keys or recovery seed phrase is crucial. Store these backups in a secure location, preferably offline. In addition, always be cautious of phishing attacks, where malicious actors attempt to trick you into revealing your private keys or login credentials. Double-check URLs and only access your wallet through official channels to avoid falling victim to such attacks.

It is essential for the safety of your wallet that you always keep all of your software and applications up to date. Updates are frequently released by developers in order to fix security issues. Moreover, consider diversifying your holdings across different wallets and types to add an extra layer of security. A combination of hot wallets (online) and cold wallets (offline) can balance accessibility and security.

Having a recovery plan in place is essential in the unfortunate scenario that you misplace your wallet and cannot access its contents. Ensure you have access to your backup private keys or recovery seed phrase and follow the wallet provider's instructions for recovery. Stay informed about the crypto community's latest security trends, vulnerabilities, and updates to ensure you're constantly employing the best security practices.

In conclusion, the protection of your assets in alternative cryptocurrencies is a duty that calls for thoughtful deliberation and active steps to be taken. You may considerably lower the chance of losing your digital assets to cybercriminals by using the right type of wallet, according to recommended procedures, diversifying your holdings, and keeping up with the most recent developments in the field of information security. In the ever-changing landscape of cryptocurrencies, protecting your investments through robust security measures is not only a prudent choice but an essential one to safeguard your financial future.

Exchanges and Trading Platforms: Buying, Selling, and Trading Altcoins

The rapidly expanding market for cryptocurrencies has resulted in the emergence of a diversified ecosystem of digital assets, each of which possesses its own set of characteristics and possible uses. Altcoins, or alternative cryptocurrencies to Bitcoin, have become a focal point for investors seeking opportunities beyond the realm of the pioneering cryptocurrency. Exchanges and trading platforms are the go-to destinations for anyone looking to access and interact with altcoins, also known as the virtual marketplaces in which these digital assets are purchased, sold, and traded. This section delves into the world of exchanges and trading platforms, exploring their functions, types, considerations, and the evolving landscape that shapes altcoin trading.

Exchanges and trading platforms serve as the gateway to the cryptocurrency market, enabling users to acquire, trade, and manage various digital assets, including altcoins. These platforms facilitate the exchange of cryptocurrencies for fiat currencies (such as the US Dollar or Euro) and other cryptocurrencies. They provide a user-friendly interface, order matching systems, and wallet functionalities that simplify engaging in cryptocurrency trading.

At their core, exchanges offer a marketplace for buyers and sellers to interact. The order book displays current buy and sell orders, and trades are executed when the bid and ask prices match. Trading platforms also offer features like trading charts, historical price data, and technical analysis tools, allowing users to make informed decisions.

Exchanges and trading platforms come in various forms, each catering to different user preferences and needs. Centralized exchanges (CEXs) are the most common type and are operated by centralized entities. They provide a user-friendly experience but require users to trust the platform's security and integrity. Well-known CEXs include Coinbase, Binance, and Kraken.

On the other hand, decentralized exchanges (DEXs) operate without a central intermediary. DEXs allow users to retain control of their private keys and funds while directly trading with one another. This model aligns with the ethos of decentralization and privacy inherent in cryptocurrencies. Platforms like Uniswap and SushiSwap exemplify the DEX concept.

Engaging in altcoin trading on exchanges and trading platforms requires careful consideration of several factors. Security is paramount, as the cryptocurrency market has seen its share of hacks and breaches. When deciding on a platform, users should place a high priority on solid security measures, such as cold storage of funds, two-factor authentication (2FA), and an established history of protecting user assets.

Liquidity is another factor to take into account; this refers to the ease with which an asset may be bought or sold without resulting in major price shifts. Established exchanges often have higher liquidity, allowing for smoother trading experiences. It's also essential to assess the range of altcoins supported by a platform, as different exchanges offer varying selections of digital assets.

The landscape of exchanges and trading platforms continues to evolve, driven by technological advancements, regulatory changes, and shifts in market demand. As governments all over the world attempt to build frameworks for cryptocurrency trading, regulatory compliance is becoming an increasingly crucial aspect of the industry. Some platforms may restrict user access from specific jurisdictions due to regulatory considerations.

Furthermore, the emergence of decentralized finance (DeFi) has spurred the growth of decentralized exchanges. DEXs offer a level of user control and autonomy that aligns with the foundational principles of cryptocurrencies. However, DEXs may also pose challenges related to user experience and liquidity.

Exchanges and trading platforms are the lifeblood of the cryptocurrency market, serving as conduits for individuals to access and engage with altcoins and other digital assets. These platforms, whether centralized or decentralized, provide users with a variety of services that are designed to meet their individual needs and interests. When considering altcoin trading, security, liquidity, and platform reputation are critical to evaluate.

As the cryptocurrency market evolves, exchanges and trading platforms will adapt to technological advancements and regulatory changes. Navigating this evolving landscape requires users to stay informed, exercise caution, and choose platforms that align with their investment goals and risk tolerance. In the realm of altcoin trading, these platforms are the portals through which individuals can participate in the transformative potential of decentralized finance and blockchain technology.

Staking and Yield Farming: Earning Passive Income with Altcoins

The world of cryptocurrencies has revolutionized finance and introduced innovative ways for individuals to generate income. Beyond traditional investments, staking and yield farming concepts have gained prominence, enabling holders of altcoins to earn passive income while playing a part in the growth and security of blockchain networks. This section delves into staking and yield farming, exploring their mechanics, benefits, risks, and the evolving landscape of passive income opportunities within the altcoin ecosystem.

Staking and yield farming are integral components of the decentralized finance (DeFi) movement, which aims to recreate traditional financial services using blockchain technology and cryptocurrencies. The act of holding and "staking" a pre-established quantity of cryptocurrency in a wallet in order to contribute to the maintenance of a blockchain network is referred to as staking. In return for providing this support, participants receive rewards in the form of additional tokens.

Yield farming, on the other hand, takes staking a step further by involving users in liquidity provision. Participants contribute their tokens to liquidity pools on decentralized exchanges (DEXs) to facilitate trading and earn a portion of the transaction fees. In return, they receive rewards in the form of interest or additional tokens from the DEX and the DeFi protocols they participate in.

Staking and yield farming offers a range of benefits to altcoin holders and participants in the DeFi ecosystem. One of the primary advantages is the opportunity to earn passive income. By staking or providing liquidity, individuals can generate returns on their holdings without actively trading. This aligns with the broader trend of decentralized finance, which aims to democratize financial services and put control back in the hands of individuals.

Additionally, staking and yield farming contributes to the security and functionality of blockchain networks. Stakers play a vital role in validating transactions and maintaining network integrity. By providing liquidity, yield farmers enhance the efficiency and liquidity of decentralized exchanges, contributing to a more vibrant trading ecosystem.

While staking and yield farming offer enticing benefits, they also come with risks and considerations that participants should be aware of. One of the primary risks is related to the cryptocurrency market's volatility. The value of altcoins can fluctuate significantly, impacting the overall value of rewards earned through staking or yield farming. Participants should carefully assess their risk tolerance and consider diversifying their investments.

Furthermore, the DeFi space is relatively young and rapidly evolving. The risks of smart contract vulnerabilities, protocol failures, and regulatory changes should not be underestimated. Due diligence is essential when selecting the platforms and protocols to participate in. Researching the track record of projects, auditing processes, and community engagement can help mitigate these risks.

The landscape of passive income opportunities within the altcoin ecosystem is dynamic and continually evolving. Staking and yield farming are just the tip of the iceberg. DeFi protocols continue to innovate, introducing new ways for individuals to earn passive income. Concepts like liquidity mining, where participants provide liquidity for specific tokens to earn rewards, and algorithmic stablecoins, which incentivize users to hold tokens that aim to maintain a stable value, are gaining traction.

Furthermore, integrating different blockchains and the rise of cross-chain solutions offer opportunities for participants to stake or provide liquidity across multiple networks. This interoperability expands the potential for earning passive income and diversifying one's strategy.

Staking and yield farming represents a transformative shift in how individuals can generate passive income within the altcoin ecosystem. Beyond traditional investments, these concepts empower individuals to actively participate in blockchain networks' growth, security, and functionality. The benefits of earning passive income while contributing to decentralized finance are compelling but not without risks.

As the landscape of DeFi continues to evolve, participants should stay informed, exercise caution, and choose platforms and protocols that align with their investment goals and risk tolerance. Staking and yield farming are windows of opportunity that enable individuals to be more than passive holders of altcoins; they become active contributors to the decentralized economy, shaping the future of finance through their participation.

Participating in Token Sales as well as Initial Coin Offerings (ICOs)

In cryptocurrency, innovative fundraising methods have emerged to support blockchain projects and startups. Among these methods, Initial Coin Offerings (ICOs) and token sales have garnered significant attention as avenues for individuals to participate in early-stage investment opportunities. ICOs revolutionized the fundraising landscape by allowing projects to issue and distribute their own digital tokens to backers in exchange for funds.

ICOs and token sales are fundraising mechanisms through which blockchain projects and startups raise capital by issuing and selling their own digital tokens to the public. These tokens often serve as utility or functional tokens within the project's ecosystem, granting holders access to the platform's specific features, services, or benefits. ICOs typically occur during the early stages of a project's development, providing contributors with an opportunity to support the project's vision and growth.

Participating in ICOs and token sales involves several steps. First, thorough research of the project's whitepaper, team members, technology, use case, and market potential is crucial. Before considering an investment, an informed understanding of the project's fundamentals is necessary. Once the research is complete, participants can send cryptocurrency (such as Ethereum or Bitcoin) to the project's designated wallet address to purchase tokens. In return, they receive the project's tokens at a predetermined exchange rate. It's essential to ensure that a compatible wallet is set up to receive the purchased tokens. After the ICO concludes, the tokens are distributed to participants' wallets, and the project often lists the tokens on cryptocurrency exchanges to facilitate trading and liquidity.

Participating in ICOs and token sales offers several potential benefits. First and foremost, ICOs provide an opportunity to invest in promising projects during their early stages. Successful projects may experience significant value appreciation over time, leading to potential profits for early contributors. Additionally, participants gain access to innovative blockchain projects that may introduce groundbreaking technologies or solve real-world challenges. Moreover, the tokens acquired through ICOs may have functional utility within the project's ecosystem, granting holders access to specific services, features, or benefits that further enhance the value proposition.

While ICOs hold promise, they also come with risks that participants should consider. One significant risk is the lack of regulation that characterized the early days of ICOs. This led to cases of fraud and scams, highlighting the need for participants to exercise caution and perform due diligence. Moreover, the value of tokens acquired through ICOs can be highly volatile. The market for cryptocurrencies is widely recognized for its swift price changes, which can affect the worth of investments. Furthermore, not all projects that conduct ICOs succeed. Before committing funds, participants should carefully assess the project's feasibility, team credibility, and market potential.

The regulatory landscape surrounding ICOs varies by jurisdiction. Some countries have embraced ICOs under specific regulatory frameworks, while others have imposed restrictions or outright bans. Participants should be aware of the legal environment in their region and choose ICOs that comply with local regulations. This awareness is crucial to ensure that participants are not inadvertently engaging in activities that could result in legal consequences.

To navigate ICOs effectively, participants should adopt strategic approaches that maximize the potential benefits while minimizing risks. Diversification is an essential strategy, as it helps avoid putting all funds into a single ICO. Participants can lessen the likelihood of losing funds due to the failure of any one project if their investments are distributed across a number of different projects. Thorough due diligence is paramount. Participants should thoroughly research the project, team, technology, and market potential before making an investment decision. It's essential to avoid making investment choices based solely on hype or FOMO (Fear of Missing Out). Instead, participants should approach decisions rationally and clearly understand the project's fundamentals. Timing is another crucial factor in the cryptocurrency market.

Participating in an ICO's early stages can secure better exchange rates and terms than participating later.

In conclusion, Initial Coin Offerings (ICOs) and token sales have revolutionized fundraising in the cryptocurrency space, offering individuals the chance to support innovative blockchain projects and gain early exposure to potential technological disruptors. While the benefits are alluring, participants must approach ICOs cautiously, conducting thorough research, assessing risks, and considering regulatory implications. By adopting a strategic and informed approach, participants can navigate the world of ICOs and potentially capitalize on early-stage investment opportunities that shape the future of the blockchain ecosystem.

CHAPTER VI

The Future of Altcoins and Emerging Trends

DeFi (Decentralized Finance) and Altcoins: Transforming Traditional Finance

The emergence of blockchain technology as well as cryptocurrencies has resulted in a dramatic transformation of the existing structure of the global financial system. Decentralized Finance, commonly known as DeFi, has emerged as a powerful force reshaping traditional financial systems. Simultaneously, the rise of alternative coins, or altcoins, has expanded the cryptocurrency ecosystem beyond the boundaries set by Bitcoin. This section delves into the profound impact of DeFi and altcoins on finance, exploring their transformative potential, challenges, and implications for the future.

DeFi signifies a paradigm shift in the way financial services are thought of and carried out. DeFi does away with the need for intermediaries like banks, brokers, or any other conventional financial institutions because it is built on blockchain platforms like Ethereum. Instead, it employs smart contracts to create a trustless and permissionless environment for various financial activities, including lending, borrowing, trading, and more. This fundamentally alters the power dynamics of finance, democratizing access and control over financial resources.

One of the groundbreaking aspects of DeFi is its inclusivity. Traditional financial services often exclude a significant portion of the global population due to stringent eligibility criteria, lack of access, and high fees. DeFi allows unbanked or underbanked individuals to participate in financial activities on an equal footing. For instance, individuals in developing countries can use DeFi platforms to secure loans without needing a credit history, thereby fostering economic empowerment.

Despite its transformative potential, DeFi has challenges. The sector has grappled with security vulnerabilities in smart contracts, regulatory uncertainties, and scalability concerns. High-profile hacks of DeFi protocols have highlighted the importance of robust security measures and audits. Additionally, regulatory bodies are still grappling with how to classify and oversee DeFi projects, which often transcend geographical boundaries. As the technology matures, balancing innovation and regulatory compliance will be crucial for DeFi's sustainable growth.

Altcoins, a term for any cryptocurrency other than Bitcoin, have diversified and expanded the cryptocurrency ecosystem. While Bitcoin remains the flagship cryptocurrency, altcoins bring unique features and use cases to the table. Ethereum, often considered the pioneer of smart contracts, laid the foundation for many DeFi applications. Other altcoins, such as Ripple (XRP), focus on enabling seamless cross-border payments, while Litecoin (LTC) emphasizes fast and low-cost transactions.

These altcoins not only showcase the technical versatility of blockchain technology but also cater to specific niches and user preferences. They facilitate experimentation with new consensus mechanisms, governance models, and scalability solutions. However, the proliferation of altcoins also raises concerns about oversaturation, market speculation, and the potential for value dilution. Some altcoins might struggle to find genuine utility beyond their initial hype, leading to a boom and bust cycle.

The interplay between DeFi and altcoins is noteworthy. DeFi platforms often rely on specific altcoins as collateral, governance tokens, or reward mechanisms. This symbiotic relationship fosters a dynamic ecosystem where innovations in DeFi can drive the demand for certain altcoins and vice versa. As both concepts evolve, their convergence could lead to even more sophisticated financial applications, potentially challenging the dominance of traditional finance.

The transformative potential of DeFi and altcoins extends beyond the current state of affairs. If harnessed effectively, they could lead to a financial system that is more efficient, transparent, and accessible. DeFi's automated and decentralized nature could streamline processes and reduce the reliance on intermediaries prone to inefficiencies. On the other hand, Altcoins might unlock new avenues for value transfer, investment, and asset tokenization.

However, realizing this potential requires addressing the challenges head-on. Regulatory clarity is essential to provide a stable environment for innovation and adoption. Technological advancements like Ethereum's transition to a proof-of-stake consensus mechanism could enhance scalability and sustainability. Moreover, fostering financial literacy and education about DeFi and altcoins is crucial to empower users to make informed decisions and mitigate risks.

In conclusion, DeFi and altcoins are two intertwined forces reshaping traditional finance and cryptocurrency. DeFi's ability to provide financial services without intermediaries aligns with the ethos of decentralization, enabling greater inclusivity and control. Altcoins, with their diverse functionalities, enhance the capabilities of blockchain technology and cater to a wide array of user needs. As these concepts evolve, their collaborative potential could revolutionize how we perceive, access, and engage with financial services. However, this transformation hinges on overcoming technical, regulatory, and adoption challenges, paving the way for a more decentralized and democratized financial future.

NFTs (Non-Fungible Tokens) and Altcoins: The Digital Ownership Revolution

With the inception of blockchain technology, the digital world has undergone a remarkable transformation that has given rise to unique ideas like Non-Fungible Tokens (NFTs) and Altcoins. While Altcoins, which include all cryptocurrencies other than Bitcoin, diversify the cryptocurrency ecosystem, NFTs offer a paradigm shift in how we view and validate ownership of digital assets. This section delves into the profound impact of NFTs and Altcoins on the realm of digital ownership, exploring their transformative potential, challenges, and implications for the future.

NFTs have emerged as a groundbreaking innovation within the realm of blockchain technology. Unlike cryptocurrencies like Ethereum or Bitcoin, which are fungible and interchangeable, NFTs are unique and indivisible. Each NFT represents ownership of a specific digital item, whether it's digital art, collectibles, virtual real estate, or even tweets. The concept of NFTs addresses a long-standing challenge in the digital age: establishing true ownership and scarcity in a world of easily replicable digital content.

One of the most remarkable features of NFTs is their ability to enable creators and artists to monetize their digital works directly. Through the mechanism of smart contracts, artists can embed royalties into their NFTs, ensuring that they receive a percentage of future sales whenever the NFT changes hands. This can potentially revolutionize the creative industry, empowering artists to have more control over their work and monetization strategies. It also introduces a new level of transparency, as ownership and transaction history of NFTs are recorded on the blockchain, providing an immutable provenance record.

However, the NFT ecosystem has its challenges. Environmental concerns have arisen due to the energy-intensive nature of blockchain networks, particularly for proof-of-work-based systems like Ethereum. As the popularity of NFTs grows, so does the carbon footprint associated with their creation and trading. Additionally, the hype around NFTs has led to concerns about speculative bubbles and the potential for value manipulation. Ensuring that the NFT market matures sustainably and responsibly will be crucial for its long-term viability.

Altcoins, encompassing all cryptocurrencies besides Bitcoin, play a vital role in the cryptocurrency ecosystem by diversifying use cases and functionalities. While Bitcoin remains the flagship cryptocurrency and store of value, altcoins bring unique technical features and applications to the table. Ethereum, for instance, introduced the concept of smart contracts, which laid the foundation for the NFT boom. Other altcoins, like Ripple (XRP), focus on facilitating frictionless cross-border payments, while Cardano (ADA) emphasizes a scientific and research-driven approach to blockchain development.

The proliferation of altcoins has led to an experimentation-rich environment where different consensus mechanisms, governance models, and scalability solutions are explored. However, the abundance of altcoins also raises concerns about market saturation and the potential for value dilution. Not all altcoins will achieve long-term success or find meaningful utility beyond their initial hype, leading to a cycle of innovation, speculation, and consolidation.

The relationship between NFTs and altcoins is multifaceted. Many NFT platforms and marketplaces operate using specific altcoins for transactions and fees. As the NFT market expands, certain altcoins may find increased demand as the preferred currency for NFT-related activities. Similarly, some NFT projects issue their tokens as a form of governance and utility within their ecosystems, tying NFTs and altcoins even closer together.

The transformative potential of NFTs and altcoins extends beyond their current applications. NFTs could revolutionize ownership not only in the digital realm but also in physical assets. Real estate, luxury goods, and even intellectual property could be tokenized as NFTs, enabling fractional ownership and streamlined transfer of value. On the other hand, Altcoins could lead to new paradigms of financial systems, decentralized applications, and innovative services.

To realize this potential, the challenges must be met head-on. The environmental impact of blockchain networks needs to be mitigated by adopting more energy-efficient consensus mechanisms or transitioning to proof-of-stake systems. Regulatory clarity is essential to ensure that NFTs and altcoins can operate within legal frameworks, promoting innovation while safeguarding consumers. Moreover, fostering digital literacy and educating users about the benefits and risks of NFTs and altcoins is crucial to empower individuals to make informed decisions.

In conclusion, NFTs and altcoins are two transformative forces reshaping the digital ownership landscape and the broader cryptocurrency ecosystem. NFTs introduce a new digital asset ownership validation and monetization paradigm, fostering transparency and empowering creators. Beyond Bitcoin, Altcoins enhance blockchain technology's capabilities by offering diverse functionalities and use cases. Their synergistic relationship has the potential to redefine how we perceive, trade, and own assets in the digital age. However, realizing this potential requires addressing technical, environmental, regulatory, and adoption challenges, paving the way for a more decentralized and digitized future.

Interoperability and Cross-Chain Solutions: Bridging Different Blockchains

The proliferation of blockchain technology has given rise to various blockchain networks, each with unique features, protocols, and functionalities. However, this fragmentation has led to isolated ecosystems, hindering the seamless exchange of assets and information. Interoperability and cross-chain solutions have emerged as essential concepts in the blockchain space, aiming to bridge the divide between different blockchains and unlock their full potential. This section delves into the significance of interoperability, explores the challenges and solutions to achieving it, and discusses the implications for the future of blockchain technology.

The term "interoperability" describes how well several blockchain networks can connect, share information, and carry out transactions. To fully realize the disruptive promise of blockchain technology, interoperability is essential in a fragmented blockchain landscape where each network runs independently. Interoperability enables the efficient exchange of assets, information, and value across diverse blockchain ecosystems, fostering collaboration, innovation, and inclusivity.

One of the key motivations behind interoperability is the need for fluid asset movement. Transferring assets from one blockchain to another often requires complex and time-consuming processes involving multiple intermediaries and exchanges. Interoperability solutions aim to simplify this process, allowing users to move assets between blockchains with ease. This has profound implications for sectors such as finance, supply chain management, and digital identity, where the ability to transfer assets and data across different platforms is crucial.

Achieving interoperability in the blockchain space is not without its challenges. The decentralized and consensus-driven nature of blockchains, while ensuring security and trust, can complicate efforts to establish seamless connections between networks. Technical differences in consensus mechanisms, smart contract languages, and underlying protocols pose hurdles in achieving true interoperability.

In order to overcome these challenges, several distinct approaches have been suggested. One common method is using middleware protocols that act as bridges between blockchains. These protocols facilitate the transfer of assets and data between blockchains, often utilizing pegged assets or wrapped tokens. Another approach involves sidechains, which are parallel blockchains that are interoperable with the main chain. Sidechains can execute specific tasks more efficiently while maintaining a connection to the main blockchain.

Additionally, projects are developing cross-chain communication protocols that enable blockchains to exchange information in a standardized and secure manner. These protocols ensure compatibility and security while allowing different blockchains to communicate and collaborate without compromising their respective autonomy.

The implications of achieving interoperability extend far beyond technical considerations. Interoperability has the potential to reshape industries and foster innovation on a global scale. For instance, the finance sector could benefit from cross-chain solutions that enable the seamless transfer of assets and liquidity between different blockchain networks, paving the way for more efficient and inclusive financial services.

Supply chain management is another domain where interoperability could drive transformative change. With interoperable blockchains, supply chain stakeholders could track and verify the journey of goods across different networks, enhancing transparency, traceability, and accountability.

Moreover, interoperability could enable the creation of decentralized applications (dApps) that span multiple blockchains. Many dApps are confined to a single blockchain platform, limiting their capabilities. With interoperability, developers could leverage the strengths of different blockchains to create more versatile and robust applications.

While the potential benefits of interoperability are vast, several challenges must be addressed as the technology evolves. Security remains a primary concern when establishing connections between blockchains, as vulnerabilities in one chain could compromise others in the network. Ensuring the integrity and confidentiality of cross-chain transactions is paramount.

Additionally, achieving consensus on interoperability standards is essential to avoid fragmentation and guarantee seamless communication between blockchains. Different blockchain communities may have varying philosophies and priorities, making finding common ground to enable interoperability crucial.
As blockchain technology evolves, interoperability will be pivotal in shaping its trajectory. Collaborative efforts, standardization, and the development of robust cross-chain solutions will be critical in creating a cohesive and interconnected blockchain ecosystem.

Interoperability and cross-chain solutions hold the key to unlocking the full potential of blockchain technology. By enabling seamless communication and asset exchange between different blockchain networks, interoperability can reshape industries, enhance collaboration, and drive innovation. While challenges exist, the concerted efforts of blockchain developers, researchers, and stakeholders are paving the way for a future where blockchains can work together harmoniously, transcending boundaries and limitations. As blockchain technology continues to mature, interoperability will remain a driving force in realizing the transformative impact of decentralized systems on various sectors of the global economy.

Environmental Concerns and Altcoins: The Shift to Proof of Stake

The cryptocurrency market's rapid growth has brought unprecedented opportunities and challenges. Among these challenges, environmental concerns have emerged as a prominent issue due to the energy-intensive nature of many blockchain networks, particularly those relying on the proof-of-work (PoW) consensus mechanism. As the demand for sustainability increases, the shift towards proof of stake (PoS) consensus mechanisms for altcoins has gained momentum. This section explores the environmental impact of blockchain networks, the advantages of PoS over PoW, the challenges in transitioning, and the implications of this shift for the broader cryptocurrency ecosystem.

Blockchain networks, which underpin cryptocurrencies like Bitcoin and altcoins, operate through complex consensus mechanisms that require significant computational power. PoW, the original consensus mechanism, relies on miners solving difficult mathematical puzzles to validate transactions and add blocks to the blockchain. This process demands vast amounts of energy, leading to concerns about carbon emissions, resource consumption, and their contribution to climate change.

As the pioneering cryptocurrency, Bitcoin has been the primary target of environmental criticism due to its high energy consumption. The process of "mining" new Bitcoins requires powerful computers competing to solve complex equations, consuming enormous electricity resources. Estimates of Bitcoin's annual energy consumption rival that of entire countries, sparking debates on the sustainability of blockchain technology.

PoS has emerged as an energy-efficient alternative to PoW in response to environmental concerns. PoS operates by validators staking a certain amount of cryptocurrency as collateral, which is then used to secure and validate transactions. Validators are chosen to create new blocks based on factors like their stake and the age of their holdings, eliminating the need for resource-intensive computations.

The advantages of PoS over PoW are multifold. First and foremost, PoS significantly reduces energy consumption. Since validators are not engaged in solving complex mathematical problems, the energy requirements of PoS networks are orders of magnitude lower. Second, PoS systems offer faster transaction confirmation times and increased scalability, making them suitable for high-throughput applications. Lastly, PoS aligns incentives toward network security, as validators have a stake in the network's success.

While the advantages of PoS are clear, transitioning from PoW to PoS is challenging. Technical complexities, resistance to change, and concerns over security and decentralization have slowed down the adoption of PoS mechanisms. PoW-based networks are deeply entrenched in the cryptocurrency ecosystem, and transitioning to PoS requires careful planning and stakeholder consensus.

One challenge is the initial distribution of wealth and stake. PoS mechanisms allocate block creation based on existing holdings, which can lead to a concentration of power among those already possessing significant amounts of cryptocurrency. Balancing decentralization with economic incentives is a complex task that requires innovative solutions.

Security is another concern. PoS networks rely on validators who must lock up a certain amount of cryptocurrency as collateral. This introduces the risk of "nothing at stake" attacks, where validators can attempt to confirm multiple conflicting transactions without facing the costs associated with PoW mining. Mitigating these risks through protocol design and economic incentives is crucial.

The shift to PoS has significant implications for the broader cryptocurrency ecosystem. Beyond its environmental benefits, PoS mechanisms can lead to increased participation, as the barrier to entry is lowered compared to PoW mining. This could foster a more inclusive and diverse network of validators and stakeholders.

Moreover, PoS mechanisms could facilitate the adoption of blockchain technology in sectors where sustainability is a priority, such as supply chain management, renewable energy trading, and carbon offset markets. PoS networks' energy efficiency aligns with the goals of these industries, potentially driving adoption and innovation.

The environmental concerns associated with blockchain networks, particularly those using PoW mechanisms, have spurred discussions and actions toward a more sustainable future for cryptocurrencies. The shift to PoS mechanisms represents a promising solution, offering energy efficiency, scalability, and increased participation. While challenges exist in transitioning and security, the momentum towards PoS is a positive step towards creating a greener and more inclusive cryptocurrency ecosystem.

As the world grapples with environmental challenges, the cryptocurrency industry has an opportunity to be a part of the solution by embracing sustainable technologies. PoS mechanisms and other innovations in the blockchain space can reduce energy consumption and drive the adoption of decentralized systems in sectors where sustainability is a paramount concern. The transition to PoS represents a fundamental shift in the landscape of altcoins and the broader cryptocurrency ecosystem, paving the way for a more responsible and eco-friendly digital future.

CHAPTER VII

Risks and Challenges of Altcoin Investing

Volatility and Price Fluctuations: Managing Investment Risks

Cryptocurrency investing has rapidly evolved, with a diverse array of digital assets known as altcoins emerging alongside the pioneering Bitcoin. While altcoins offer exciting investment opportunities and novel use cases, they also come with inherent risks, particularly in price volatility and fluctuations. This section delves into the significance of volatility in altcoin investing, explores strategies for managing investment risks, and discusses the implications for investors and the broader cryptocurrency ecosystem.

The degree to which an asset's price fluctuates over a specified time period is referred to as the asset's volatility. In the context of altcoin investing, volatility is a defining characteristic due to many cryptocurrencies' nascent and speculative nature. Unlike traditional financial markets, where regulatory mechanisms and established institutions can mitigate extreme price swings, the cryptocurrency market operates with a higher level of unpredictability.

The reasons behind the high volatility of altcoins are multifaceted. Relatively low market capitalization, shallow liquidity, and the absence of intrinsic value anchors can all contribute to rapid price movements. Moreover, the market sentiment surrounding cryptocurrencies is highly sensitive to news, regulatory developments, and technological advancements, amplifying price fluctuations.

While volatility presents challenges, it also offers opportunities for savvy investors who can effectively manage risks. Diversification is a cornerstone strategy in altcoin investing. Spreading investments across different cryptocurrencies can help mitigate the impact of a single asset's price decline. This approach reduces the risk of a significant loss while potentially capitalizing on the growth of multiple assets.

Thorough research and due diligence are crucial for identifying altcoins with solid fundamentals and promising use cases. Understanding the technology, team, partnerships, and market trends can help investors make informed decisions. Additionally, setting clear investment goals and timeframes can assist in navigating short-term volatility while staying focused on long-term potential. Risk

management extends beyond individual altcoins to overall portfolio management. Allocating a portion of the portfolio to more stable assets, such as established cryptocurrencies like Bitcoin or Ethereum, can act as a hedge against extreme price fluctuations in altcoins. Moreover, employing tools like stop-loss orders can limit potential losses by automatically selling an asset if its price drops below a predetermined level.

The implications of managing volatility in altcoin investing are profound for individual investors and the broader cryptocurrency ecosystem. For investors, understanding and effectively navigating volatility can result in substantial gains. However, it requires patience, research, risk management, and a long-term perspective.

From a macro perspective, managing volatility is crucial for the overall credibility and adoption of the cryptocurrency ecosystem. Excessive price volatility can deter mainstream adoption and investment, as businesses and individuals may be hesitant to engage with assets prone to extreme price swings. Additionally, regulatory scrutiny can increase if volatile price movements are perceived as a threat to financial stability.

Volatility and price fluctuations are integral elements of the altcoin investing landscape. While they present challenges, they also offer opportunities for strategic investors who can manage risks effectively.

Diversification, due diligence, risk management tools, and a long-term perspective are vital strategies for navigating altcoins' dynamic and often unpredictable world.

Addressing volatility as the cryptocurrency market evolves becomes pivotal for fostering broader adoption and institutional participation. Efforts to increase stability, liquidity, and regulatory clarity can contribute to a more mature and resilient cryptocurrency ecosystem. While the journey to managing volatility in altcoin investing may be tumultuous, it is a vital step towards realizing the transformative potential of blockchain technology and the digital assets it has spawned.

Regulatory Uncertainty: Navigating Legal and Compliance Issues

The world of altcoin investing has emerged as a dynamic and promising arena for individuals and institutions seeking exposure to the evolving landscape of blockchain technology. However, alongside the opportunities, regulatory uncertainty has cast a shadow over the altcoin market. As governments and regulatory bodies grapple with defining the legal status of digital assets, investors face complex challenges in navigating legal and compliance issues. This section delves into the significance of regulatory uncertainty in altcoin investing, explores strategies for managing compliance risks, and discusses the implications for investors and the broader cryptocurrency ecosystem.

The regulatory landscape for cryptocurrencies and altcoins is characterized by its complexity and variability. Different jurisdictions adopt diverse approaches to classifying and regulating digital assets, ranging from outright bans to embracing them as legitimate financial instruments. This regulatory diversity has created a landscape where altcoin investors must navigate a patchwork of laws, regulations, and guidelines.

The lack of a universal legal framework for altcoins stems from several factors. Cryptocurrencies challenge traditional notions of currency, securities, and commodities, blurring the lines between existing regulatory categories. Additionally, the rapid pace of technological innovation has left regulatory bodies struggling to keep up with the evolving nature of digital assets.

In the face of regulatory uncertainty, investors must adopt proactive strategies to manage compliance risks. Firstly, understanding the regulatory environment in one's own jurisdiction is crucial. Staying informed about regulatory developments and seeking legal counsel can help investors assess the legal implications of their altcoin investments.

Furthermore, adopting a risk-based approach to investment decisions can mitigate potential compliance issues. Investing in well-established and reputable altcoins with transparent teams and clear use cases may reduce the likelihood of regulatory scrutiny. Conducting thorough due diligence on altcoin projects and their compliance efforts can provide insights into their commitment to regulatory alignment.

The implications of navigating regulatory uncertainty in altcoin investing are far-reaching. For investors, compliance risks extend beyond financial penalties to potential asset freezes, legal battles, and reputational damage. Regulatory scrutiny can lead to restrictions on trading, withdrawal delays, and even the delisting of altcoins from exchanges.

At the macro level, regulatory uncertainty affects the overall credibility and adoption of the cryptocurrency ecosystem. Institutions, including traditional financial players, often hesitate to engage with altcoins due to concerns about regulatory clarity and compliance risks. This hesitancy can limit mainstream adoption and dampen investment flows into the altcoin market.

As the altcoin market continues to evolve, the role of regulatory clarity cannot be overstated. Clear and consistent regulations provide a foundation of trust and stability for investors and businesses operating within the cryptocurrency ecosystem. Regulatory clarity can attract institutional investors, facilitate innovation, and promote healthy competition among altcoin projects.

Collaboration between the cryptocurrency industry and regulatory bodies is essential for achieving regulatory clarity. Industry players can contribute their expertise to shape regulations that balance innovation and investor protection. Regulatory sandboxes, which allow projects to operate within controlled environments while testing new technologies, can serve as valuable testing grounds for mutually beneficial regulations.

Regulatory uncertainty poses a multifaceted challenge for altcoin investors and the broader cryptocurrency ecosystem. The necessity for a regulatory framework that is both transparent and standardized is becoming ever more pressing due to the continued rise in popularity of digital assets. Investors must adopt a proactive and informed approach to navigate compliance risks while the cryptocurrency industry and regulatory bodies collaborate to balance innovation and investor protection.

Achieving regulatory clarity requires a collective effort that involves stakeholders from various sectors, including government, industry, and academia. By fostering an environment of dialogue, cooperation, and transparency, the cryptocurrency ecosystem can evolve into a mature and responsible space that welcomes innovation, safeguards investors, and contributes to the broader transformation of global finance and technology.

Market Saturation and Project Failures: Picking Winners in a Crowded Market

The altcoin market has flourished recently, with a proliferation of digital assets beyond the pioneering Bitcoin. This growth has brought opportunities and challenges, one of the most prominent being market saturation and the potential for project failures. Navigating a crowded market to identify promising altcoin investments is daunting, requiring careful analysis, due diligence, and an understanding of the factors contributing to project success or failure. This section explores the significance of market saturation and project failures in altcoin investing, examines strategies for selecting winners in a competitive landscape, and discusses the implications for investors and the broader cryptocurrency ecosystem.

As the altcoin market expands, it becomes increasingly saturated with many projects competing for attention, funding, and adoption. This saturation can lead to a dilution of value, where the sheer number of projects makes it difficult for any single one to stand out. Investors face the challenge of differentiating between genuinely promising projects and those that lack substance, putting their capital at risk in a crowded and competitive landscape.

The ease of launching new altcoins exacerbates market saturation. Blockchain technology has lowered the barriers to entry, allowing almost anyone with technical knowledge to create a new cryptocurrency. This has led to many projects, some lacking a clear use case, innovative technology, or a dedicated team.

The prevalence of market saturation increases the likelihood of project failures, where altcoins fail to deliver on their promises or gain meaningful adoption. Project failures can result from various factors, including technical shortcomings, poor execution, lack of market fit, and failure to attract users or investors.

Investors in altcoins face substantial risks when backing projects that ultimately fail. Capital invested in failed projects can be lost entirely, leading to financial losses and dashed expectations. Moreover, project failures can erode trust in the broader altcoin ecosystem, dampening investor sentiment and limiting the growth of innovative and legitimate projects.

Selecting winners in a crowded market requires a combination of strategic approaches and due diligence. One essential strategy is conducting thorough research on altcoin projects. Understanding the project's technology, use case, team background, and market positioning can help investors gauge the project's potential for success.

Analyze the project's roadmaps and whitepapers critically. Projects with well-defined roadmaps, achievable milestones, and transparent communication are more likely to follow through on their promises. Similarly, well-documented whitepapers that outline the project's technical aspects, goals, and value proposition indicate a thoughtful and credible project.

Investors should also consider the project's community engagement and partnerships. An active and engaged community can contribute to the project's success by fostering adoption and driving innovation. Partnerships with established companies, organizations, or industry players can lend credibility to the project and expand its reach.

Diversification remains a prudent strategy in a crowded market. Spreading investments across multiple altcoins can help mitigate risks associated with individual project failures. However, diversification should be combined with thorough research to avoid investing in subpar projects.

The implications of navigating market saturation and project failures in altcoin investing are profound for both investors and the broader cryptocurrency ecosystem. For investors, the risks of investing in underperforming projects highlight the importance of due diligence, informed decision-making, and risk management. Project failures can lead to financial losses, disillusionment, and a cautious approach toward future investments.

Market saturation and project failures can hinder the industry's progress in the broader cryptocurrency ecosystem. Failures can erode investor trust and confidence, making it more difficult for legitimate projects to secure funding and gain traction. This can slow down innovation, limit investment flows, and create a challenging environment for projects with genuine potential.

Market saturation and project failures are inherent challenges in the dynamic world of altcoin investing. The growing number of altcoin projects competing for attention makes it essential for investors to adopt a cautious and informed approach. Thorough research, critical analysis, and an understanding of the factors contributing to project success can help investors navigate the crowded landscape and identify projects with genuine potential.

For the cryptocurrency ecosystem to thrive, stakeholders must collectively work towards establishing transparency, accountability, and credibility standards. While market saturation may persist, a commitment to quality projects, responsible investing practices, and continuous improvement can contribute to developing a more mature, innovative, and resilient altcoin ecosystem.

Psychological Traps: Overcoming FOMO and Panic Selling

With its potential for rapid gains and losses, the altcoin market has become a captivating arena for investors seeking opportunities in the cryptocurrency ecosystem.

However, along with the prospects of profit, the world of altcoin investing presents psychological challenges that can lead to impulsive decisions with adverse consequences. Two significant psychological traps that altcoin investors often fall into are the Fear of Missing Out (FOMO) and panic selling. This section explores the significance of FOMO and panic selling in altcoin investing, examines strategies for overcoming these psychological traps, and discusses the implications for investors and the broader cryptocurrency ecosystem.

FOMO is a psychological phenomenon that compels individuals to make hasty decisions driven by the fear of missing out on potential gains. In the context of altcoin investing, FOMO often arises when investors witness sudden price surges in certain coins or witness others profiting from their investments. FOMO-driven decisions can lead to impulsive purchases at inflated prices without thorough research or considering long-term prospects.

The altcoin market's volatility amplifies the impact of FOMO. Investors who succumb to FOMO may chase after rapidly appreciating coins, only to experience abrupt price reversals and losses. This behavior can contribute to creating speculative bubbles and heightened market volatility.

Overcoming FOMO requires a disciplined and informed approach to altcoin investing. Setting clear investment goals and risk thresholds can help investors make rational decisions aligned with their financial objectives. Developing and sticking to a solid investment strategy can mitigate the influence of FOMO-induced impulses. Thorough research is a crucial defense against FOMO. Conducting due diligence on altcoin projects, and evaluating their technology, team, use case, and market potential can help investors make knowledgeable decisions based on fundamental factors rather than emotional impulses. Furthermore, avoiding short-term price charts and focusing on the project's long-term viability can reduce the susceptibility to FOMO-driven trading.

Panic selling occurs when investors react impulsively to short-term market downturns, often triggered by fear and uncertainty. Panic selling can lead to significant losses in the altcoin market, where prices can experience swift and substantial fluctuations. Emotional reactions to market events can cloud judgment and lead to hasty decisions that investors later regret.

Panic selling can exacerbate market downturns. When many investors engage in panic selling simultaneously, it can amplify price drops, creating a self-fulfilling cycle of fear and more selling. This dynamic contributes to market volatility and undermines the stability of the altcoin ecosystem.

Overcoming panic selling requires cultivating emotional resilience and adopting a long-term perspective. Developing an investment plan with risk management strategies can help investors maintain their composure during market downturns. Setting stop-loss orders at reasonable levels can buffer against extreme price drops while allowing for healthy market fluctuations.

Investors can also benefit from seeking rational advice during market turbulence. Engaging with a reliable network consisting of peers, mentors, or financial professionals can provide helpful insights and combat the need to make decisions based only on emotions. Additionally, detaching from short-term price movements and focusing on the underlying fundamentals of the altcoin project can help investors weather market volatility.

The implications of overcoming FOMO and panic selling extend beyond individual investors to the broader cryptocurrency ecosystem. Emotion-driven trading behavior can lead to market inefficiencies and erratic price movements, undermining the credibility of the altcoin market. Unpredictable behavior can deter institutional adoption and hinder the establishment of a mature and stable cryptocurrency ecosystem.

When looking at investing from the perspective of an individual investor, it is crucial to avoid falling into psychological traps in order to maintain a sound and sustainable investment approach. The altcoin market's potential for gains and losses demands a disciplined mindset prioritizing research, risk management, and a long-term perspective over impulsive reactions.

FOMO and panic selling are psychological traps that altcoin investors must navigate in the dynamic and volatile cryptocurrency market. Overcoming these traps requires a combination of strategic approaches and emotional discipline. Thorough research, a solid investment plan, rational advice-seeking, and a focus on long-term fundamentals can help investors counteract emotional impulses and make informed decisions.

Investors' responsible behavior is crucial for the broader cryptocurrency ecosystem to thrive. Investors can contribute to a more stable, credible, and innovative altcoin ecosystem by overcoming psychological traps. As the market matures, fostering an environment of informed decision-making, rational trading, and emotional resilience will be pivotal in realizing the transformative potential of blockchain technology and the digital assets it has spawned.

CHAPTER VIII

Developing an Altcoin Investment Strategy

Short-Term vs. Long-Term Investing: Choosing Your Approach

The world of altcoin investing is characterized by its dynamism, rapid price fluctuations, and the potential for substantial gains and losses. Within this dynamic landscape, investors face a crucial decision: whether to adopt a short-term or long-term approach to their altcoin investments. Both approaches have their merits and challenges, and choosing between them can significantly impact an investor's risk tolerance, goals, and overall strategy. This section explores the significance of short-term and long-term investing in altcoins, examines the advantages and disadvantages of each approach, and discusses the implications for investors and the broader cryptocurrency ecosystem.

Short-term investing in altcoins involves capitalizing on price volatility to make quick profits over a relatively brief period. Traders adopting this approach often engage in day trading or swing trading, aiming to profit from short-lived price movements. The fast-paced nature of short-term investing requires constant monitoring of the market and swift execution of trades.

One of the primary advantages of short-term investing is the potential for rapid gains. Short-term traders can benefit from both upward as well as downward price movements in a volatile market by correctly identifying market trends. Additionally, short-term trading can provide an avenue for gaining experience and learning about market dynamics, contributing to a trader's skill development.

However, short-term investing also comes with challenges. The constant need to monitor the market and make quick decisions can be mentally taxing, leading to stress and burnout. Moreover, transaction fees, taxes, and potential losses due to incorrect predictions can eat into profits. Short-term traders may also miss out on the long-term growth potential of altcoins by focusing solely on immediate price movements.

Long-term investing in altcoins involves holding assets for an extended period, often measured in months or years. Long-term investors prioritize the potential for significant growth over time and are less concerned with short-term price fluctuations. This approach requires patience, a strong belief in the long-term potential of the invested assets, and a willingness to withstand temporary market downturns.

The primary advantage of long-term investing is the potential for substantial returns if an altcoin's value appreciates significantly over time. Investors identifying fundamentally strong projects with promising use cases and technology may benefit from participating in the altcoin's growth trajectory. Long-term investors also benefit from reduced stress and decision fatigue, as they are less affected by short-term price volatility.

However, long-term investing has its challenges. Holding assets over extended periods requires commitment and the ability to weather market downturns without succumbing to panic selling. Additionally, long-term investors run the risk of holding assets that fail to gain traction or deliver on their promises, resulting in losses over time.

The choice between short-term and long-term investing in altcoins is profoundly personal and should be aligned with an investor's financial goals, risk tolerance, and time availability. Short-term investing may appeal to those who enjoy the excitement of quick trades and have the time and resources to constantly engage with the market.

Long-term investing, on the other hand, may suit individuals who prefer a more passive approach, are patient, and believe in the potential of their chosen projects.

Short- and long-term investors play essential roles for the broader cryptocurrency ecosystem. Short-term traders contribute to market liquidity and price discovery, while long-term investors provide stability and support the growth of projects over time.

The decision between short-term and long-term investing in altcoins is a pivotal choice that shapes an investor's strategy, risk exposure, and potential outcomes. While short-term investing offers the allure of quick gains, it comes with constant monitoring and decision-making challenges. Long-term investing provides the prospect of significant growth over time but requires patience and conviction to weather market fluctuations.

Ultimately, there is no one-size-fits-all approach to altcoin investing. Before making a choice, investors should carefully assess their objectives, level of risk tolerance, and time horizon. Moreover, a balanced approach combining short-term and long-term strategies can provide a diversified and well-rounded investment portfolio.

As the altcoin market evolves, short-term and long-term investors contribute to its vibrancy and growth. By embracing the strengths of each approach and aligning them with individual preferences, investors can navigate the dynamic world of altcoin investing while contributing to the development of a resilient and transformative cryptocurrency ecosystem.

Dollar-Cost Averaging: Mitigating the Impact of Market Volatility

The altcoin market, characterized by its volatility and potential for rapid price fluctuations, presents opportunities and challenges for investors seeking to navigate this dynamic landscape. One of the strategies that have gained popularity in mitigating the impact of market volatility is dollar-cost averaging (DCA). Regardless of the asset's valuation, DCA entails making recurring investments of a defined amount of money. This strategy strives to lessen the effects of short-term market swings and offer a structured and methodical means to accumulate alternative currencies over time. This section explores the significance of dollar-cost averaging in altcoin investing, examines its advantages and limitations, and discusses the implications for investors and the broader cryptocurrency ecosystem.

Dollar-cost averaging is a strategy that prioritizes consistency over timing when investing. Instead of attempting to predict market highs and lows, investors allocate a fixed amount of capital at predefined intervals, such as weekly, monthly, or quarterly. Regardless of whether the altcoin's price is high or low at the time of investment, the investor acquires a predetermined amount of the asset.

The idea of purchasing more units of an asset when prices are low and less of it when prices are high forms the foundation of DCA. This strategy seeks to lessen the danger of making poor investments based on short-term price fluctuations over time and balance out the effects of market volatility.

Dollar-cost averaging offers several advantages for altcoin investors, especially in a market known for its price volatility. One of the key benefits is risk reduction. By spreading out investments over time, investors are less exposed to the risk of making significant investments at a time when prices are at their peak. This helps in avoiding the emotional pitfalls of trying to time the market.

Furthermore, DCA provides a disciplined approach to investing. It removes the need for investors to monitor price movements and make impulsive decisions constantly. This can reduce stress and decision fatigue, allowing investors to concentrate on the long-term potential of their altcoin investments.

While DCA is a valuable strategy for mitigating the impact of market volatility, it has limitations. One of the primary drawbacks is the potential for missed opportunities during periods of rapid price appreciation. If an altcoin experiences a sudden and sustained price increase, investors employing DCA might accumulate fewer units than those who made a lump-sum investment early on.

Additionally, DCA may not be suitable for all investors or all market conditions. Some investors might prefer a more active approach that capitalizes on short-term price movements. Furthermore, in a market where the overall trend is consistently downward, DCA might not be the most effective strategy for accumulating altcoins, as the value of the investment could decrease over time.

The implications of employing dollar-cost averaging in altcoin investing extend to both individual investors and the broader cryptocurrency ecosystem. For investors, DCA offers a systematic and disciplined approach that reduces the emotional impact of market volatility. It encourages a long-term perspective and discourages rash decision-making driven by short-term price movements.

From the perspective of the cryptocurrency ecosystem, DCA can contribute to market stability. As more investors adopt this strategy, the likelihood of extreme price fluctuations caused by panic selling or irrational buying behavior decreases. A more stable market environment can attract institutional investors and foster mainstream adoption of altcoins.

Dollar-cost averaging is a powerful strategy for mitigating the impact of market volatility in the altcoin investing landscape. By removing the pressure to time the market and providing a disciplined approach to accumulation, DCA offers investors a practical way to navigate the dynamic world of cryptocurrency. While it might not be suitable for all investors or market conditions, DCA provides a valuable tool for those seeking to minimize the risks associated with the high volatility of the altcoin market.

As the cryptocurrency ecosystem evolves, strategies like dollar-cost averaging contribute to a more informed, responsible, and resilient investment approach. By focusing on the long-term potential of altcoins and employing strategies that prioritize consistency and discipline, investors can contribute to developing a mature and credible cryptocurrency market that benefits individual participants and the broader global economy.

Setting Realistic Goals and Expectations: Patience in Altcoin Investing

With its potential for rapid gains and losses, the world of altcoin investing can be both exhilarating and daunting for investors. Amidst the excitement, one of the most critical aspects of successful altcoin investing is setting realistic goals and expectations. Patience, often regarded as a virtue, is pivotal in navigating the volatile altcoin market. This section explores the significance of setting realistic goals and expectations in altcoin investing, delves into the advantages of a patient approach, and discusses the implications for investors and the broader cryptocurrency ecosystem.

Setting realistic goals and expectations is fundamental to a well-structured investment strategy. In the altcoin market, where price movements can be swift and unpredictable, clearly understanding what one hopes to achieve is crucial for making informed decisions. Realistic goals help investors remain grounded and avoid impulsive actions driven by fear, greed, or the desire for quick gains.

Moreover, realistic expectations foster emotional resilience. By acknowledging the inherent volatility of the altcoin market, investors are better prepared to weather price fluctuations without losing sight of their long-term objectives. In this context, patience is closely intertwined with setting realistic goals and expectations.

A patient approach to altcoin investing offers several advantages that contribute to sustainable growth and prudent decision-making. One of the primary benefits is reduced emotional stress. The altcoin market's volatility can evoke a range of emotions, from euphoria during price surges to panic during downturns. A patient mindset helps investors maintain composure and make rational choices, regardless of short-term price movements.

Patience also allows investors to reap the benefits of compounding over time. Investors can benefit from the possibility for exponential growth as altcoins increase in value by committing to a long-term strategy. This patient approach aligns with the adage that "time in the market is more important than timing the market."

While setting realistic goals and expectations is essential, determining the appropriate timeframes for these goals is equally important. Different investors may have varying time horizons based on their financial objectives, risk tolerance, and life circumstances. Some may be comfortable with a short- to medium-term horizon, seeking to capitalize on shorter price movements, while others may have a longer-term perspective, focusing on the potential for significant growth over several years.

It's important to note that the altcoin market's dynamics can influence the pace of achieving one's goals. Investors should be prepared for unexpected market developments and adjustments to their investment strategies as new information becomes available.

The implications of setting realistic goals and expectations extend to both individual investors and the broader cryptocurrency ecosystem. From an individual investor's perspective, aligning goals with expectations and adopting a patient approach fosters a disciplined and informed investment strategy. Patience helps investors avoid making rash decisions based on short-term price movements, increasing the likelihood of achieving long-term financial objectives.

A collective commitment to setting realistic goals and expectations can contribute to the cryptocurrency ecosystem's stability and credibility. Investors who adopt a patient approach are less likely to contribute to market volatility through panic selling or speculative trading. A more stable and rational market environment is conducive to attracting institutional investors and mainstream adoption of altcoins.

Setting realistic goals and expectations while embracing patience is a cornerstone of successful altcoin investing. The altcoin market's volatility necessitates a disciplined and informed approach that considers both short-term price movements and long-term growth potential. Investors can navigate the altcoin landscape with confidence and resilience by setting clear objectives, understanding the market's dynamics, and maintaining patience.

In an era where the cryptocurrency ecosystem is rapidly evolving, informed and patient investors contribute to its maturation and credibility. By setting the example of rational decision-making, a long-term perspective, and the cultivation of patience, individual investors are vital in shaping the future of altcoin investing and the broader global financial landscape.

Rebalancing Your Portfolio: Adapting to Changing Market Dynamics

The world of cryptocurrency investing, particularly in altcoins, is marked by its dynamic and often volatile nature. In this evolving landscape, portfolio rebalancing is one of the key strategies for achieving long-term success. Rebalancing involves adjusting the composition of a portfolio to ensure that it aligns with an investor's desired risk and return profile. This section explores the significance of portfolio rebalancing in altcoin investing, delves into the benefits and considerations of this strategy, and discusses the implications for investors and the broader cryptocurrency ecosystem.

Portfolio rebalancing is a proactive strategy that aims to maintain an investor's desired asset allocation, even as market conditions change. In the context of altcoin investing, rebalancing involves periodically reviewing the distribution of assets within a portfolio and making adjustments to realign with the investor's original allocation targets.

For example, suppose an investor initially allocated 60% of their portfolio to altcoins and 40% to more stable assets like Bitcoin. In that case, market fluctuations might cause the altcoin portion to grow to 70% due to altcoin price appreciation. Rebalancing would involve selling some of the altcoins and buying more Bitcoin to return the portfolio to the desired 60/40 allocation.

Portfolio rebalancing offers several benefits contributing to a disciplined and informed investment approach. One of the primary advantages is risk management. By rebalancing, investors can mitigate the impact of extreme price movements in a single asset class. This diversification helps reduce the potential for significant losses during market downturns while allowing investors to participate in the growth potential of various assets.

Furthermore, rebalancing allows investors to capitalize on market trends and capture profits. When an asset class experiences substantial appreciation, rebalancing involves selling a portion of the appreciated asset and buying assets that have not performed as well. This "buy low, sell high" approach aligns with sound investment principles and can contribute to overall portfolio growth.

While portfolio rebalancing is a valuable strategy, it requires careful consideration and an understanding of an investor's individual goals and risk tolerance. The frequency of rebalancing depends on various factors, including the volatility of the assets, an investor's time horizon, and the desired level of involvement in managing the portfolio.

Additionally, investors should assess transaction costs and tax implications when rebalancing. Frequent rebalancing can lead to increased transaction fees and potential tax consequences. Balancing these costs with the benefits of maintaining a well-diversified and aligned portfolio is essential.

The implications of portfolio rebalancing extend to individual investors and the broader cryptocurrency ecosystem. For investors, rebalancing offers a systematic approach to maintaining a well-diversified portfolio and managing risk. This disciplined strategy helps investors avoid emotional decision-making pitfalls and minimizes short-term market fluctuations' impact.

In the cryptocurrency ecosystem, portfolio rebalancing contributes to market stability. As more investors adopt rebalancing strategies, the likelihood of excessive price volatility caused by herd behavior or speculative trading decreases. A stable and rational market environment can attract institutional investors and support the growth of altcoins as a legitimate asset class.

Portfolio rebalancing is a dynamic and essential strategy for altcoin investors seeking to navigate the ever-changing landscape of cryptocurrency investing. By adjusting asset allocations in response to market dynamics, investors can maintain a diversified and aligned portfolio that are in line with their financial objectives and risk tolerance. This disciplined approach offers benefits such as risk management, capturing profits, and avoiding emotional decision-making.

As the cryptocurrency ecosystem evolves, portfolio rebalancing is crucial in shaping a responsible and informed investment approach. By embracing strategies prioritizing diversification, risk management, and disciplined decision-making, investors contribute to developing a resilient and credible altcoin market. Through portfolio rebalancing, investors adapt to changing market conditions, increase their chances of long-term success, and actively participate in the transformative potential of blockchain technology and digital assets.

CHAPTER IX

Case Studies: Successful Altcoin Investors

Individuals Who Profited from Altcoin Investments

Cryptocurrency has been a realm of innovation, volatility, and transformative potential. Within this dynamic landscape, individuals from various walks of life have ventured into altcoin investments with remarkable success. These individuals, often referred to as early adopters or crypto pioneers, have navigated the complexities of the altcoin market to achieve substantial profits. This section delves into the stories of individuals who profited from altcoin investments, exploring their journeys, strategies, and the implications of their success for the broader cryptocurrency ecosystem.

The Winklevoss Twins: Pioneering Institutional Adoption

Cameron and Tyler Winklevoss, famously known as the Winklevoss twins, epitomize early adoption and success in the altcoin market. The Winklevoss brothers, most known for their court dispute with Mark Zuckerberg over the launch of Facebook, switched to cryptocurrencies and established the Gemini exchange in 2014.

The twins invested heavily in Bitcoin during its early days, accumulating a substantial amount of the cryptocurrency. Their foresight and conviction in the potential of cryptocurrencies paid off handsomely as Bitcoin's value soared over the years. Furthermore, they were instrumental in advocating for the institutionalization of the cryptocurrency market, working towards regulatory compliance and security measures that helped pave the way for mainstream adoption.

Erik Finman: From Teenager to Bitcoin Millionaire Erik

Finman's story is a testament to the democratizing potential of cryptocurrencies. At the age of 12, Finman invested a gift of $1,000 from his grandmother into Bitcoin just a few years after its inception. His investment proved to be a wise move, as Bitcoin's value skyrocketed in the following years.

Finman's journey from a teenage Bitcoin enthusiast to a millionaire is a remarkable tale of how small investments can lead to significant gains in the cryptocurrency market. His success also highlights the importance of early adoption and the potential for individual investors to benefit from emerging technologies.

Barry Silbert: A Visionary Investor

Barry Silbert is a prominent figure in the cryptocurrency space, renowned for his role in founding Digital Currency Group (DCG) in 2015. DCG is a venture capital company that has invested in many blockchain and cryptocurrency projects, making Silbert an influential player in the industry.

Silbert's early investments in Ethereum and Zcash have yielded substantial returns. His foresight in identifying promising projects and his ability to invest in them strategically have contributed to his success in the altcoin market. Additionally, Silbert's efforts to promote innovation and foster collaboration within the cryptocurrency ecosystem have impacted the industry's development.

Tim Draper: The Bitcoin Auction Winner

Due to his successful participation in a U.S. government auction of seized Bitcoin, venture capitalist and founder of Draper Associates, Tim Draper gained attention in the cryptocurrency world. In 2014, Draper purchased nearly 30,000 Bitcoins from the auction, a move that was met with skepticism at the time due to the prevailing uncertainty surrounding cryptocurrencies.

Draper's investment paid off spectacularly as Bitcoin's value surged over the years. His foresight and willingness to take risks in an emerging and uncharted market underscore the potential rewards for individuals open to exploring new opportunities.

Brian Armstrong: Building a Cryptocurrency Empire One of the largest and most recognized digital currency exchanges in the world, Coinbase, was co-founded by Brian Armstrong, who additionally functions as its CEO. Under Armstrong's leadership, Coinbase has played a pivotal role in bringing cryptocurrencies to mainstream audiences and facilitating their adoption.

Armstrong's success extends beyond his role as the head of Coinbase. As an advocate for the cryptocurrency ecosystem, he has contributed to the growth of altcoins and the broader blockchain technology space. His commitment to education, transparency, and regulatory compliance has been instrumental in shaping the cryptocurrency landscape.

The success stories of individuals profiting from altcoin investments offer valuable insights and lessons for investors and the broader cryptocurrency ecosystem. These stories highlight the importance of early adoption, foresight, and a willingness to explore emerging technologies.

For individual investors, these success stories underscore the potential rewards of altcoin investments. While the altcoin market carries inherent risks and uncertainties, the stories of those who achieved substantial profits inspire diligent research, informed decision-making, and a long-term perspective.

On a larger scale, the success of these individuals contributes to the credibility and mainstream adoption of cryptocurrencies. Their efforts in advocating for regulatory compliance, security measures, and technological innovation have paved the way for institutional participation and integration of cryptocurrencies into traditional financial systems.

The stories of individuals profiting from altcoin investments represent diverse backgrounds, strategies, and contributions to the cryptocurrency ecosystem. These success stories highlight the transformative potential of cryptocurrencies and the opportunities they offer for those willing to explore and invest in emerging technologies. As the cryptocurrency landscape continues to evolve, the lessons from these individuals' journeys inspire investors, advocates, and innovators who are shaping the future of finance and technology.

Lessons Learned and Strategies for Success

The world of altcoin investing, with its potential for rapid gains and losses, has captivated the imagination of investors worldwide. Amidst the excitement and volatility of this dynamic landscape, valuable lessons can be learned from the experiences of those who have navigated the altcoin market successfully. This section delves into the lessons learned and strategies for success from altcoin investors, exploring their insights, challenges, and the implications for both individual investors and the broader cryptocurrency ecosystem.

One of the fundamental lessons from successful altcoin investors is the importance of conducting thorough research before making investment decisions. In the realm of altcoins, where projects vary in quality and potential, informed decision-making hinges on a deep understanding of a project's technology, use case, team, and market potential.

Investors like Mark Cuban have emphasized the significance of the research, cautioning against investing in projects solely based on hype or trends. The experiences of successful investors highlight the value of taking the time to delve into whitepapers, evaluate roadmaps, and assess the credibility of development teams. This strategy helps investors separate promising projects from those lacking substance, ultimately contributing to a well-informed and rational investment approach.

Diversification is a principle that transcends traditional investment markets and holds significant importance in the altcoin landscape. Successful altcoin investors emphasize the benefits of spreading investments across various projects rather than concentrating resources on a single asset. Diversification helps manage risk and allows investors to capitalize on the growth potential of different altcoins.

Lessons from experienced investors underscore the importance of striking a balance between established cryptocurrencies like Bitcoin and Ethereum and newer, emerging altcoins. By diversifying across well-established and promising projects, investors can participate in various stages of growth and innovation within the altcoin ecosystem.

Volatility is an inherent characteristic of the altcoin market, and navigating it requires a long-term perspective. Successful investors stress the importance of maintaining patience and avoiding the pitfalls of emotional decision-making driven by short-term price movements. Focusing on the long-term potential of altcoins allows investors to weather market fluctuations while capturing growth opportunities.

The experiences of individuals like the Winklevoss twins highlight the rewards of holding onto investments through market cycles. Their commitment to Bitcoin paid off handsomely as its value appreciated over time. This lesson underscores the potential benefits of holding altcoins with solid fundamentals and growth potential, even in the face of short-term uncertainty.

Altcoin investing is not without risks, and successful investors stress the importance of setting clear objectives and risk limits. Defining investment goals, risk tolerance, and exit strategies helps investors avoid succumbing to emotional impulses during market volatility. Moreover, risk management strategies like setting stop-loss orders provide a safety net against significant losses.

The experiences of individuals like Tim Draper, who strategically acquired a substantial amount of Bitcoin during a government auction, demonstrate the role of risk management in achieving successful outcomes. Draper's calculated approach to seizing opportunities within a high-risk environment illustrates the importance of informed decision-making and risk mitigation.

The altcoin market constantly evolves, and successful investors stress the need to stay informed and adapt to changing dynamics. Monitoring market trends, technological developments, and regulatory changes allows investors to make knowledgeable decisions and adjust their strategies accordingly.

Investors like Brian Armstrong, the CEO of Coinbase, exemplify the value of staying informed and adaptable. Armstrong's role in leading one of the world's largest cryptocurrency exchanges requires a deep understanding of the industry's trends and challenges. His ability to adapt to evolving market conditions has contributed to the growth of Coinbase and its role in mainstreaming cryptocurrency adoption.

The lessons learned and strategies for success from altcoin investors carry implications for individual investors and the broader cryptocurrency ecosystem. Investors can draw inspiration from these lessons to develop a disciplined and informed investment approach that prioritizes research, diversification, risk management, and a long-term perspective.

For the cryptocurrency ecosystem, the practices of successful investors contribute to its maturation and credibility. As more investors adopt strategies aligned with research, diversification, and risk management, the market becomes less susceptible to irrational behavior and extreme price fluctuations. A stable and informed market environment is conducive to attracting institutional investors and fostering mainstream adoption of altcoins.

The lessons learned and strategies for success from altcoin investors reflect the diverse experiences and insights of those who have navigated the complexities of the cryptocurrency landscape. Investors can navigate the altcoin market with greater confidence and resilience by conducting thorough research, diversifying investments, adopting a long-term perspective, managing risk, and staying informed.

As the cryptocurrency ecosystem evolves, the lessons from successful investors contribute to its responsible and sustainable growth. Individual investors play a pivotal role in shaping the future of finance and technology by embracing principles that prioritize rational decision-making, adaptability, and a commitment to innovation. Through these lessons, investors can achieve their financial goals and contribute to the broader transformative potential of blockchain technology and digital assets.

Mistakes to Avoid: Learning from the Challenges Faced by Early Investors

The world of altcoin investing, characterized by its potential for significant gains and losses, has attracted the attention of investors seeking to capitalize on the transformative potential of cryptocurrencies. However, the journey of early investors in altcoins was not without its challenges and pitfalls. Their experiences offer valuable insights into the mistakes that can be made when navigating the volatile altcoin market. This section delves into the mistakes to avoid, drawing lessons from the challenges faced by early investors, exploring their stories, and discussing the implications for current and future altcoin investors.

One of the most common mistakes made by early investors in altcoins was a lack of thorough research and due diligence. The excitement surrounding the emerging cryptocurrency market led some investors to dive into projects without fully understanding their technology, use case, or market potential. As a result, investments were made based on hype rather than informed decision-making.

The experiences of early investors underscore the importance of conducting extensive research before investing in any altcoin project. Investors should delve into whitepapers, assess the credibility of development teams, and evaluate the feasibility of the project's goals. By avoiding the mistake of neglecting research, investors can make more knowledgeable and rational investment decisions.

Fear of missing out (FOMO) was prevalent among early altcoin investors, driving impulsive investment decisions. The fear that missing out on the next big thing could lead to regret pushed some investors to make hasty investments without a clear understanding of the project's fundamentals. Emotional investing based on FOMO often led to losses when projects fail to deliver on their promises.

The experiences of those who fell victim to FOMO highlight the importance of emotional discipline in altcoin investing. Investors should strive to make decisions based on rational analysis rather than succumbing to emotional impulses. Setting clear objectives and risk limits can help mitigate the influence of FOMO and prevent costly mistakes.

Early altcoin investors often concentrated their investments on a single project, neglecting risk management and diversification principles. The allure of potentially astronomical gains from a single project overshadowed the importance of spreading investments across multiple assets. As a result, losses from a single project's failure were magnified.

The experiences of these investors emphasize the need for a balanced and diversified investment strategy. Diversification assists manage risk by reducing the impact of losses from a single asset. By allocating investments across a range of altcoins with different growth potentials, investors can protect their portfolios from the adverse effects of project failures.

In the early days of altcoin investing, regulatory considerations were often overlooked. Some investors failed to recognize the legal and regulatory risks of investing in unregulated or poorly compliant projects. As a result, investments were made in projects that later faced legal challenges or regulatory crackdowns.

The experiences of these investors highlight the importance of understanding the regulatory landscape in the altcoin market. Regulatory compliance can significantly impact the success and legitimacy of an altcoin project. Investors should prioritize projects that are transparent about their compliance efforts and are proactive in adhering to relevant regulations.

Early altcoin investors often lacked the patience to weather market fluctuations and nurtured their investments over time. The allure of quick profits led some investors to engage in short-term trading and speculative behavior. This approach resulted in missed opportunities for long-term growth and a heightened susceptibility to market volatility.

The experiences of early investors underscore the value of patience in altcoin investing. Rather than succumbing to short-term focus and impulsive trading, investors should adopt a long-term perspective that allows them to capture the potential growth of altcoins over time. Patience also helps investors avoid emotional reactions to market fluctuations.

The mistakes made by early investors in altcoins offer valuable lessons for current and future investors in the altcoin market. These lessons highlight the importance of conducting thorough research, managing emotions, diversifying investments, considering regulatory factors, and adopting a patient approach.

By learning from the challenges faced by early investors, individuals entering the altcoin market today can make more informed and responsible investment decisions. Applying these lessons helps investors avoid the mistakes that led to losses and setbacks in the past. Furthermore, these lessons contribute to a more mature and informed investor community that is better equipped to navigate the complexities of the altcoin market.

The mistakes made by early investors in altcoins serve as cautionary tales for anyone seeking to venture into cryptocurrency investing. The experiences of those who neglected research, succumbed to emotional impulses, disregarded risk management, ignored regulations, and lacked patience underscore the potential pitfalls of the altcoin market. By heeding these lessons, current and future investors can cultivate a disciplined, informed, and responsible investment approach that are in line with their financial goals and risk tolerance. By committing to avoiding these mistakes, investors contribute to developing a credible, resilient, and transformative altcoin ecosystem.

CONCLUSION

The Ongoing Evolution of Altcoins and Their Role in the Crypto Space

The cryptocurrency landscape has undergone a remarkable transformation since the advent of Bitcoin in 2009. While Bitcoin laid the foundation for decentralized digital currency, the introduction of altcoins brought about a new era of innovation, diversity, and experimentation. Altcoins, or alternative cryptocurrencies, have evolved to encompass many projects with distinct features, use cases, and goals. This section delves into the ongoing evolution of altcoins, exploring their historical development, the diversity of altcoin projects, their significance in the broader cryptocurrency ecosystem, and the implications for the future of finance and technology.

The term "altcoin" emerged as a portmanteau of "alternative" and "coin," referring to any cryptocurrency other than Bitcoin. The first altcoin, Namecoin, was launched in 2011 as a decentralized domain registration system built on the same codebase as Bitcoin. Namecoin's introduction marked the beginning of a wave of altcoin creations, each with its unique features and purposes.

The subsequent years witnessed the launch of altcoins like Litecoin, which aimed to enhance cryptocurrencies' scalability and transaction speed. Litecoin's success demonstrated that altcoins could offer innovative solutions while expanding digital currencies beyond Bitcoin's pioneer status.

The ongoing evolution of altcoins has given rise to an impressive array of projects that go beyond traditional digital currencies. Altcoins now encompass a broad spectrum of functionalities, including smart contract platforms, privacy-focused coins, stablecoins, decentralized finance (DeFi) tokens, and more. Each altcoin project is driven by specific goals and innovations, contributing to the diversification of the cryptocurrency ecosystem.

For example, Ethereum, launched in 2015, introduced the notion of smart contracts and decentralized applications (DApps). This groundbreaking innovation opened the door to a new wave of blockchain-based solutions, enabling developers to create programmable and self-executing agreements on the Ethereum network. Altcoins like Monero and Zcash focused on enhancing privacy features, addressing transaction traceability and user anonymity concerns.

Altcoins play a crucial role in shaping the cryptocurrency ecosystem by fostering innovation, competition, and market diversity. Their diversity allows investors and users to choose from various projects that align with their preferences and needs. This healthy competition encourages developers to continuously improve their technologies and propose new solutions to existing challenges.

Furthermore, altcoins contribute to the experimentation and evolution of blockchain technology. Projects like Cardano and Polkadot aim to enhance interoperability between blockchains, enabling the seamless exchange of information and value across different networks. DeFi altcoins have revolutionized traditional financial services by providing decentralized alternatives to banking, lending, and trading.

The ongoing evolution of altcoins holds profound implications for the future of finance, technology, and beyond. Altcoins are driving the development of innovative applications that extend far beyond simple digital transactions. As blockchain technology matures, altcoins are likely to become a key component of the broader digital economy, offering solutions that transform industries such as supply chain management, healthcare, gaming, and more.

Moreover, altcoins challenge traditional financial systems by introducing decentralized and permissionless alternatives. The rise of stablecoins pegged to real-world assets, such as the US Dollar or commodities, has the potential to close the gap between traditional and digital finance. This innovation could lead to greater financial inclusion, especially in regions with limited access to conventional banking services.

The ongoing evolution of altcoins is a testament to the revolutionary power of blockchain technology and decentralized innovation. From their humble beginnings as alternatives to Bitcoin, altcoins have grown into a diverse ecosystem of projects encompassing various functionalities and use cases. The ongoing development of altcoins continues to drive innovation, competition, and experimentation in cryptocurrency.

As altcoins evolve and contribute to the expansion of blockchain technology, their role in the broader digital economy becomes increasingly significant. They challenge traditional financial paradigms, promote financial inclusion, and offer solutions to some of the world's most pressing challenges. Altcoins are shaping the future of finance and technology and redefining our understanding of how decentralized systems can reshape industries and empower individuals on a global scale.

Embracing Altcoins as a Part of Your Investment Journey

The world of finance has experienced a dramatic shift with the emergence of cryptocurrencies and blockchain technology. While Bitcoin, as the first and most well-known cryptocurrency, laid the foundation for this digital revolution, the introduction of altcoins has brought new dimensions to the investment landscape. Altcoins, or alternative cryptocurrencies, offer a diverse range of opportunities beyond Bitcoin. This section explores the journey of embracing altcoins as a part of your investment strategy, delving into the motivations, considerations, strategies, and potential benefits of incorporating altcoins into your portfolio.

The decision to embrace altcoins as a part of your investment journey often stems from a combination of motivations. Traditional investments like stocks and bonds may offer stability, but the allure of high growth potential in the cryptocurrency market draws investors seeking to diversify their portfolios and capture new opportunities. Altcoins offer an avenue to invest in emerging technologies and innovative projects that have the potential to disrupt various industries.

Additionally, the decentralized nature of cryptocurrencies aligns with a desire for financial sovereignty and autonomy. The prospect of participating in a global financial system that operates outside traditional institutions is appealing to those who value transparency, security, and control over their assets.

Before incorporating altcoins into your investment strategy, several considerations merit careful attention. Altcoins are associated with greater volatility than traditional assets, making risk management a paramount concern. Research becomes a cornerstone of your approach, as understanding each altcoin's technology, use case, team, and market potential is essential for informed decision-making.

Furthermore, regulatory considerations must be considered. The regulatory landscape surrounding cryptocurrencies varies by jurisdiction and can impact the legality and acceptance of specific altcoins. Staying informed about regulations and compliance efforts is crucial to ensure a smooth and compliant investment journey.

Embracing altcoins as a part of your investment journey requires a strategic approach tailored to your risk tolerance, investment goals, and time horizon. Diversification is a key strategy, spreading investments across different altcoins to mitigate risk and capture potential growth. A diverse portfolio can encompass established altcoins like Ethereum, which offer robust ecosystems and utility, and newer projects with innovative features.

The role of timing must be considered. The volatility of the altcoin market means that timing your investments strategically can yield significant benefits. Taking advantage of market trends, emerging technologies, and project developments can enhance the potential returns on your investment.

Embracing altcoins as a part of your investment journey presents a range of potential benefits. First and foremost is the opportunity for substantial returns. Altcoins have demonstrated the potential to deliver significant gains over relatively short periods. Early investments in projects with solid fundamentals and growth potential can lead to substantial profits.

Moreover, altcoins expose a diverse range of use cases and industries. Projects like Chainlink, which focuses on decentralized oracle networks, or Polkadot, which aims to enhance blockchain interoperability, highlight the breadth of innovation within the altcoin space. Investing in projects aligned with your interests and convictions allows you to contribute to and participate in technological advancements beyond financial gain.

Embracing altcoins as a part of your investment journey is a decision that reflects the transformative potential of cryptocurrencies and the evolving landscape of finance. While the allure of high returns and innovative technologies draws investors, the journey requires careful consideration, research, and strategic planning. Diversification, risk management, and regulation compliance are vital elements to address.

As the altcoin market continues to evolve, embracing altcoins can open doors to new investment opportunities and participation in groundbreaking technologies. However, it is essential to approach altcoin investing with a long-term perspective, mindful of the inherent volatility and the need for informed decision-making. By understanding the motivations, conducting thorough research, and crafting a strategic approach, you can confidently navigate the altcoin landscape and position yourself to benefit from the ongoing evolution of cryptocurrencies.

Final Thoughts and Encouragement for Exploring Altcoin Opportunities

A paradigm shift is taking place in the financial industry, propelled by the emergence of cryptocurrencies and blockchain technology. Within this transformative landscape, altcoins have emerged as a dynamic and diverse set of investment opportunities, offering individuals a chance to explore new frontiers in wealth generation and technological innovation. As we conclude our exploration of altcoin opportunities, we must reflect on the journey so far, address common concerns, and encourage those considering venturing into this exciting realm.

Our journey through the world of altcoins has been an illuminating one. From understanding the historical evolution of altcoins to delving into their role in reshaping finance, we've explored the intricacies of this dynamic market. We've learned the importance of research, risk management, diversification, and strategic planning in altcoin investing. Along the way, we've encountered the challenges early investors face and the strategies successful altcoin enthusiasts employ. As we approach this exploration's conclusion, it's essential to reflect on the lessons we've learned and the implications they hold for the future.

Exploring altcoin opportunities is not without its share of concerns and hesitations. The volatility of the market, regulatory uncertainties, and the fear of missing out on probable gains can be daunting factors. However, it's essential to approach these concerns with a balanced perspective. While volatility presents risks, it also offers opportunities for those who adopt a long-term view and conduct thorough research. Regulatory uncertainties highlight the need for compliance but also reflect the evolving nature of the regulatory landscape, which can provide more clarity as the market matures.

Fear of missing out can lead to hasty decisions, but it's crucial to remember that altcoin investing is a journey, not a race. More long-term success may result from cautiously navigating the market and selecting actions that are consistent with your risk appetite and investing objectives.

As we conclude our exploration, let's take a moment to encourage those considering or already exploring altcoin opportunities. The transformative potential of altcoins lies in their potential for financial gains and their contribution to technological innovation. The altcoin space is a creative hub, where developers work on projects that address real-world challenges and reshape industries. By participating in this ecosystem, you become a part of a global movement that is pushing the boundaries of what is possible.

Embracing altcoin opportunities also means embracing education. The more you learn about blockchain technology, various altcoins, and the trends shaping the market, the more confident and informed your decisions will be. Education empowers you to cut through the noise, filter out the hype, and identify projects with genuine potential.

Furthermore, embracing altcoin opportunities requires a mindset of resilience. The journey may have its ups and downs, but the lessons learned from successful investors and the insights gained from our exploration can serve as guiding lights. Remember that altcoin investing is a marathon, not a sprint. Stay concentrated on your long-term goals, and resist the temptation to be swayed by short-term market fluctuations.

As we conclude our exploration of altcoin opportunities, it's evident that we are at the forefront of a transformative era in finance and technology. Exploring altcoins is filled with challenges, uncertainties, and opportunities. It requires a commitment to education, a patient approach, and a willingness to embrace innovation. Altcoins are not just an investment vehicle; they are a gateway to participating in the future of decentralized finance, technological advancements, and global change.

Remember that research principles, risk management, and informed decision-making are your compass amid uncertainty and excitement. You can navigate the altcoin landscape with greater confidence and resilience by grounding your choices in these principles. Whether you are just beginning your exploration or have already embarked on this journey, take heart in the knowledge that you are contributing to a movement reshaping the world as we know it. The future is yours to shape, and altcoin opportunities are the canvas on which you can paint your financial and technological aspirations.

Thank you for buying and reading/ listening to our book. If you found this book useful/ helpful please take a few minutes and leave a review on the platform where you purchased our book. Your feedback matters greatly to us.